Magna Carta

Our Shared Legacy of Liberty

John Robson

With Brigitte Pellerin

ISBN-13: 978-0-9781706-3-9

DEDICATION

To our three little production assistants.

CONTENTS

Introduction   3

Alfred the Great   10

From Saxons to Normans to Runnymede   15

Enter Bad King John   21

Stephen Langton: A Hero for Our Times   25

The Battle for Rochester Castle   28

The Star of the Show   31

The Battle for Dover Castle   33

Simon de Montfort: A Hero for Parliament   36

Liberty for the Common Man   42

Odiham Castle   46

Part II: The Triumph of Liberty   49

Parliament and Magna Carta   56

The Inns of Court   59

King Henry the Dangerous   64

The Importance of Religious Freedom   68

Edward Coke: A Hero for Magna Carta   72

A King Beheaded   85

The Founding of America   93

Magna Carta in the Colonies   97

The Ancient American Constitution   106

Canada's Ancient Constitution   110

Part III: Challenges to Liberty   113

A Duty to Remember   122

Conclusion   135

ACKNOWLEDGMENTS

This book only exists because of more than 1200 people and organizations who backed and promoted the documentary on which it is based, who are credited by name in that documentary and to whom we again express our thanks here. We are also grateful to all the organizations who let us film at various historic sites and shared their knowledge and passion for Magna Carta. And to all those, from Stephen Langton and William Marshal to the present day, who have defended and continue to defend liberty under law so there was and still is an inspiring story to tell.

Introduction

On the banks of the Thames River at Runnymede, west of London, a real-life miracle happened 800 years ago. When Bad King John was forced to put the royal seal on Magna Carta, giving constitutional protection to key human rights, it laid the foundation of the system of government we still enjoy in Canada and throughout the English-speaking world.

The key rights guaranteed in Magna Carta include a fair legal system, accessible to everyone; security of the person; protection of property; a right to a say in how you're governed; and freedom from oppressive taxation. They are remarkably modern-sounding but they are also timeless. And they are the only way ever found to build a decent society in which individuals matter.

(12) "No 'scutage' or 'aid' may be levied in our kingdom without its general consent…"

(28) No constable or other royal official shall take corn or other movable goods from any man without immediate payment, unless the seller voluntarily offers postponement of this."

(39) "No free man shall be seized or imprisoned, or stripped of his rights or possessions, or outlawed or exiled, or deprived of his standing in any other way, nor will we proceed with force against him, or send others to do so, except by the lawful judgement of his equals or by the law of the land."

(40) "To no one will we sell, to no one deny or delay right or justice."

Magna Carta is a miracle in three ways. First of all, it's extraordinary that all these key rights would find expression in one constitutional document.

It's even more extraordinary that the rights enumerated in Magna Carta were not a wish list, an expression of how people wished the world might be if only the government wasn't as wretched as it is. They were an expression of rights that really were, by and large, upheld in England even eight, nine, ten centuries ago.

And the third miraculous aspect of Magna Carta is that the protections written down at Runnymede in June 1215 were not eroded or crushed with the passing of the years and the coming and going of fads in government. Instead they were preserved, refined, expanded and enhanced over the ensuing 800 years, making possible the kind of society that we enjoy today.

The history of liberty in the Anglosphere is not one of brilliant visionaries breaking with the past to establish freedom. Nor is it a gradual evolution from a halting, limited notion of rights to an expansive and comprehensive one. Rather, it is the astonishing tale of a sound, remarkably complete system of liberty under law established a thousand years ago. And while that system was repeatedly threatened by ambitious and often cunning rulers, every time liberty was squeezed in the English-speaking world, instead of being crushed, it was forced into a harder and sharper form.

It's true that some parts of Magna Carta are as archaic as the shorthand Latin in which it was written or the sheepskin it was written on. The pledge to fire all Gerard Athee's relatives, for instance, is hardly a contemporary concern. But these specifics are woven into and derived from a general fabric of protecting life, liberty and property, for women as well as men[1], for commoners as well as nobles, of due process and popular control of the state, that are of enduring importance today in Canada and around the world.

****

It's hard to get our minds around that concept in a society obsessed with novelty, in which "medieval" is a sneering term of abuse. How could the rules that make a decent society possible have been forced upon an early 13th-century monarch by a bunch of barons who'd never seen an electric light switch, a steam engine, or a flush toilet?

The answer is that political, constitutional, and legal systems aren't like computer operating systems that need to be dramatically revised every few years or they're hopelessly, embarrassingly out of date. Their principles are timeless. And the rights contained in Magna Carta aren't just one way of creating a good society. They're the only way that's ever been found. That's why it's so important that we understand these rights, where they came from, how they flourished, and what challenges they face today.

****

We owe a great debt to the distant past here. Even Magna Carta itself was not a revolutionary document but part of the attempt, continuing into our own time, to protect the rights of citizens against government arrogance and presumption. As Daniel Hannan, Member of the European Parliament for South-East England and author of the indispensable survey *Inventing Freedom: How the English-Speaking Peoples Made the Modern World*, explains, "The easy mistake to make is to think that previous generations whose views resemble ours, they're the progressives. And the ones who are moving in the other direction, they're the reactionaries. But the fascinating thing, if you look at the debates before and up to Magna Carta, is the extent to which the people who were trying to constrain royal power saw themselves as the conservatives. They were looking, not forward to our own democratic age, but back to what they imagined to have been the natural constitution of England, one where kings were constrained, where there was a conciliar form of government, a parliamentary form, through the witan[2], and where above all, the rules were above the rulers. And here's the extraordinary thing: They were right."[3]

Magna Carta was forced upon King John, great-great-grandson of William the Conqueror, the first Norman ruler of England, by a largely

Anglo-Norman political elite. But it had its roots in Saxon England in fact and in the minds of those who confronted John at Runnymede.

When William the Conqueror invaded in 1066, he came to claim a throne, not to overthrow a political system. An important part of his assertion of legitimacy as the rightful successor to the childless Edward the Confessor, the last reigning Saxon king, was an explicit promise to his subjects to respect Edward's laws, laws that really did apply fairly to almost everyone.

In *Inventing Freedom* Hannan tells a remarkable story involving a surviving letter from Edith of Wessex, widow of Edward the Confessor, the most powerful woman in all England, "written to the court of the hundred of Wedmore in Somerset, and asking for 'a just ruling concerning Wudumann, to whom I entrusted my horses, and who has for six years withheld my rent.' We don't know which way the Wedmore court decided. But it is hard to imagine a similar case anywhere else in the world in the eleventh century."[4] Indeed, "it's  pretty hard to imagine such a thing happening in a large chunk of the world today."[5]

****

The true story of King Canute, so often mangled in modern times, also reflects the political culture of Saxon England. Though a Danish interloper, Canute was determined to be a good ruler. And when obsequious courtiers told him he was such a great king, favourite of God and all-round superior human being that he could even command the tides, Canute dragged them down to the shore to prove it was untrue. As the waves advanced despite his orders to the contrary, he rebuked his nobles both for impiety and for flattery, telling them a king needed to be told frankly what he could not or should not do if he was to govern well. It was a tale of humility in rulers that helped form the Anglosphere's conception of political leadership for over a thousand years, and we would do well to recall it now.

There's also the apocryphal story of Lady Godiva. It has persisted in folklore in large part because of her wardrobe, or rather, conspicuous lack thereof. But the point of this fanciful medieval tale about Saxon times is that Lady Godiva rode naked through the streets of Coventry to protest her own husband's excessive taxation that left the poor without food to eat or clothes to wear.

Incidentally, the phrase "peeping Tom" comes from this story; supposedly the townsfolk promised not to gawk but one tailor snuck a look and was struck blind. But the key point is that in medieval England men and women looked back to Saxon times as a period of justice and equity and humility on the part of the rulers. Moreover, they expected their rulers to do the same and behave accordingly.

Thus the most famous story handed down from Saxon times, retold and vividly remembered in the Anglosphere not just in the

Middle Ages but well into the 20th century, is that of Alfred and the Cakes. Though elements of it are again fictitious, the core of this story is true, astounding, and defining.

Alfred the Great

Alfred the Great is one of those characters in British history who, if he was invented, would be indignantly rejected as too implausible. He became king of Wessex in the darkest part of the Dark Ages after a number of his brothers had failed at the job. The kingdom was sunk in ignorance and buffeted by waves of Danish invaders.[6] Alfred himself was ambushed by the Danes at Christmastime in 877 (January 878 under the modern calendar, but under the old Julian calendar January was part of the old year), nearly killed, and fled into the marshes of Athelney. It's at this period that the almost certainly apocryphal story arises of Alfred and the cakes. But the rest of the story is real.

From a base in the marshes, Alfred rallied his own men and his allies from Mercia, defeated the Danes, forced their king to convert to Christianity, recaptured London then re-established the British navy

on a sounder footing to help fight off invaders. That alone would make him a pretty good king, and it helped inspire the American revolutionaries to name their first flagship the *USS Alfred*. But there's much, much more. Including as an adult teaching himself Latin so as to translate important books into Anglo-Saxon because he saw that learning in his kingdom had fallen into disuse.

Statue of Alfred in Winchester

There's a famous statue of Alfred in Wantage, where he was born in 849, erected on the thousandth anniversary of one of his pivotal victories over the Danes and dedicated in 1877 by the Prince of Wales (the future Edward VII). But its inscription stresses his service to learning and his piety as well as his role as a warrior. Of course schools, churches and farms must be defended with daring and determination or they will perish. But if you look at the iconography of the statue, the warrior's axe is in repose, and in his other hand is a scroll symbolizing learning and law. Alfred didn't fight because he loved battle. He fought because he loved the things soldiers must protect if they are not to be destroyed.

The iconography is equally clear in the giant statue of Alfred erected in Winchester on the thousandth anniversary of his death, in October of 1899. You can clearly see a Saxon warrior, somewhat romanticized in fact. It includes that great big beard we all know they had though what limited evidence we possess suggests Alfred was actually clean-shaven. But though he stands defiantly, sword in hand, the sword is inverted to form a cross, showing the warrior driven by piety, a man who upholds peace and learning.

There was a giant procession through Winchester before that statue was put up, an event recorded as far away as the *New York Times*. And that statue was proudly and gratefully inscribed, a thousand years after the fact, "To the founder of the kingdom and nation."

Men and women then, not a century and a half ago, were clearly not running away from their history. They even spelled Alfred A-E-L-F-R-E-D on the massive plinth. And yet that statue in the heart of historic Winchester now sits in a small and somewhat squalid car park. I fear that we're losing our sense of the magnificent past and of heroes with deeds worth emulating. And if we lose the idea, we'll lose the practice as well.

For Alfred was not merely a warrior or a scholar. Indeed, his greatest claim to fame is that he restored justice to his people and ruled humbly, respecting and enforcing the traditional laws of his people rather than arrogantly reshaping them. Which of course is the point of the parable about the cakes.

Alfred became king in 871. After winning some important victories against the marauding Danes, in late 1877 he was ambushed by the Danes at Christmastime and forced to flee into the marshes of Athelney.

There, disguised as a poor wandering man, he came and asked for refuge in a swineherd's hut. The woman didn't much like the looks of him, but since hospitality to strangers in need is a Christian duty she said, "OK, OK, come in, warm yourself by the fire, all I ask is watch the little loaves, or cakes, that I've got baking, I've got to go out and glean." Alfred sits by the fire, starts cleaning his weapons, and then he starts thinking, "How can I restore my kingdom, how do I gather my scattered Thanes, are the men of Mercia still with me?" And he gets so absorbed in these thoughts that he forgets what he's meant to be doing. Next thing you know, the hut is full of smoke, the woman is in the doorway screaming, "Why you no good bum, I let you in, I let you warm yourself, all I said is watch the cakes now they're all burned up what are we supposed to eat?" And the punchline is, instead of drawing himself up to his full regal height and saying, "Madam, you may not speak that way to your king" or swatting her head off, he apologizes. And this story, though it probably didn't really happen, was told at dinner tables and firesides in the English-speaking word for a thousand years because it embodied the expectation of political leadership, that rulers would be humble and driven by service, not arrogant and tyrannical. You just can't imagine this story existing about Louis XIV, a Russian tsar or a Japanese God-emperor. It's part of what makes the Anglosphere distinct.

The scroll at the bottom of the Winchester statue says: "Alfred found learning dead and he restored it. Education neglected and he revived it. The laws powerless and he gave them force. The Church debased and he raised it. The land ravaged by a fearful enemy, from which he delivered it." And that is why he is the one and only monarch in British history to have earned the epithet "the Great".[7]

From Saxons to Normans to Runnymede

This strong, shared understanding of the nature of their political community and their expectations of rulers permeated English political life and motivated the populace in times of crisis. Whether William had a stronger claim to the throne in 1066 than his rivals Harold Godwinson and Edgar Atheling was not something on which the typical Englishman had strong views or was eager to die. But he, and his wife, were very clear that a king who did not respect their traditional liberties forfeited his legitimacy regardless of his heredity or his designation as heir by his predecessor, and his commands might lawfully be resisted. Their new Norman overlords knew it and governed themselves accordingly.

Thus when William the Conqueror's son Henry I took the throne in 1100, having apparently bumped off his horrid brother William II in a convenient "hunting accident" following which Henry made a suspiciously prompt beeline for the royal treasury at Winchester, he too needed to establish his credentials as rightful king. So he issued a coronation charter known as the "Charter of Liberties" that, as his father had done, promised to preserve the laws of Edward the Confessor.[8]

Neither Henry nor his father were gentle men, and of course not every promise they made was meant sincerely or kept fully. But the political culture of England was such that, particularly when it came to the routine operations of government, it was necessary to preserve traditional rules or the subjects would balk or rebel. As Winston Churchill argued, its Norman overlords were never able to crush what scholars today call "civil society" and thus there was always in England, and later its overseas colonies, a "constitutional Opposition" consisting not of a court faction or political party but of alert, engaged citizens determined to protect their rights.[9] And so even in the first 150 years, between William the Conqueror and Magna Carta, as the Norman elite ruled England, quarreled among themselves, fought civil wars and raised revenue, crucial popular support went to those who preserved the basic principles of Saxon self-government.

When Henry I died without male heirs in 1135, England slipped into anarchy and war as Stephen of Blois, grandson of William the Conqueror by William's daughter Adela, tried to seize the throne from Henry's daughter Matilda. Ultimately Matilda's faction prevailed, aided by the death of Stephen's only legitimate sons during the conflict and the fact that thanks to her father's politically adept marriage, she united the Norman and Saxon royal lines. Thus when Stephen died in 1154, the throne passed to Matilda's son Henry II, the "almost great" first Plantagenet king of England.

Henry, who reigned until his death in 1189, was a willful and energetic man, master of half of France as well as of England. And he greatly improved and extended royal government in England. But he did so in a characteristic way, particularly in his establishment of a revolutionary court system that was, at its core, deeply traditional.

****

It came about because Henry was in a sometimes sordid power struggle with the nobles over who would actually administer justice. But the key to his victory wasn't brute force or low cunning. It's that he gave better justice than his rivals. And the way he did it was to increase formal popular control over law-making in England.

His technical innovation was to turn the jury, up to that point basically an instrument of royal inquiry, into a part of the court system. A group of local people would be sworn to tell the truth, not just about the facts of the case but about the law that actually existed. This system, of judgement by one's peers, was made readily available in the royal courts and the nobles could not compete with it.

Henry's royal judges "rode circuit," going to hear cases in the locality where they arose. And as they did so they delivered rulings that became precedent for future cases. But these judges *discovered* law, they didn't *make* it in the troublesome way that modern judges often do. They inquired into the rules under which the English had always agreed to live and then codified them into the famous, and unique, "common law" of England inherited by Canada outside Quebec, the United States outside Louisiana, Australia and much of the Commonwealth including India.

It can be hard to grasp this process of making law, accustomed as we are to rules emanating in huge numbers from legislatures, or indeed from bureaucracies in the form of regulations, both at the behest of a powerful executive branch with an expansive agenda for change. But law in England did not come from a parliament in the 12th century. No such legislative body existed. Nor did it come from the king, for despite popular misconceptions about oppressive and autocratic rule in medieval times, English kings had no power to make law by decree.

Quite the reverse. John of Salisbury, secretary to Archbishop of Canterbury Thomas à Becket until Becket's murder in 1170, wrote a treatise on ethics and political philosophy called *Policraticus* around 1159. And in that book he not only insisted that "The difference between the prince and the tyrant is that the prince obeys the law and governs his people in accordance with right," a claim incomprehensible, even incoherent, if the word of the prince is law. He also wrote that "not only is it lawful to slay the tyrant, but also it is right and just to do it."

****

These are not words it would have been prudent to write in France, let alone at the court of Genghis Khan. But it was the firm spirit of English political culture a century after the conquest and half a century before Magna Carta. And it resulted not only in pious statements about abstract justice but a deep-seated, extensive, flexible, effective system of common law not found anywhere else, law that genuinely emanated from the people.

During the reign of Henry II his "justiciar" Ranulf de Glanvill either wrote or had compiled a *Treatise on the Laws and Customs of England* summarizing and praising the principles of this unique and already well-developed and firmly rooted system. As Daniel Hannan notes in *Inventing Freedom*, neither the common law nor the apt alternative phrase "the law of the land" to describe it is found in other countries except those that grew out of the soil of Runnymede or had it transplanted there by those nurtured by Magna Carta. It predates anything resembling a law-making parliament. And while Henry's judges refined and expanded it, they neither created nor dramatically revised these legal rules and customs, drawn from the populace and embodying Saxon popular sovereignty.

When the Americans created a constitution in 1789 derived from "We the People", they didn't think they were innovating, and they weren't. They were deliberately preserving the vital core of a system the Normans had inherited from the Saxons. And what led directly to Magna Carta was that Henry's son John was failing to respect it. That is what made him such a bad king and led the barons, prelates, knights and common people to drag him to Runnymede to issue a formal guarantee not of new rights but of ones that were already very old eight centuries before our own time.

Enter Bad King John

Bad King John's remains lie in Worcester Cathedral in south-western England. It was one of the few places that would have him, and even they probably took him partly to make sure the lid of his coffin stayed firmly shut. He was hated and despised then, and his reputation has resisted all efforts at rehabilitation in the eight centuries since his death. Historians love revisionism, but they've never been able to pull it off with this character.

An almost contemporary chronicler, Anonymous of Bethune, described John as "brimful of evil qualities." And Mark Morris's 2015 *King John: Treachery, Tyranny and the Road to Magna Carta* asked "Did he deserve to be called 'Bad King John'? No, he was much worse than that." Another recent scholar said, "Was John really worse than his relatives? Well, we can only say that contemporaries certainly thought so. They were reluctant to fight with him, and they would not take his word without unusually strong guarantees."[10] And of course those turned out to be useless. No sooner had John sealed Magna Carta than he set about trying to break it.

King John convinced the Pope, Innocent III, to release him from his promise to uphold Magna Carta by arguing that Charter infringed

Innocent's rights as John's feudal overlord under an agreement they had made in 1213. Innocent therefore issued the papal bull[11] *Etsi karissimus* annulling Magna Carta on August 24, 1215 and excommunicating rebel barons. But all John's cunning availed him naught. Englishmen would have their rights no matter how clever or

Pope Innocent III

ruthless their king might be.

John himself raised an army, fought the barons, got sick, lost the Crown jewels in the Wash[12] and died of dysentery on October 19, 1216. Or possibly, as claimed at the time, a surfeit of peaches and new ale. Or poison. It didn't really matter.

Nobody was sorry to see him go or cared to inquire closely into the manner of his demise. And to secure the throne his young son Henry III, guided by the remarkable regent William Marshal, First Earl of Pembroke, promptly issued revised versions of Magna Carta in late

1216 and again in late 1217 (at which point the Charter of the Forest was separated out from the "Great Charter").[13]

Bad King John was gone, and Magna Carta remained. But what exactly had John been doing wrong that made him so hated, that caused so many people, great and small, to rise up against him? Simple answer, though a clichéd one: he was refusing to respect the rights of his subjects.

When John's father Henry II died in 1189, he was succeeded by John's brother Richard I, "Coeur de Lion" or "Lionheart". Despite his whitewashing in the Robin Hood legends, Richard was an outstanding military leader but a thoroughly bad king, rapacious and vainglorious, who didn't care much for England and was, indeed, buried in France. He routinely left England to go off fighting, generally with a good excuse but fundamentally because he loved fighting for its own sake, and met a thoroughly deserved end in 1199 while rampaging through Limousin in south-central France when a lucky crossbow shot winged his left shoulder and the wound turned gangrenous.

****

Richard imposed a crushing burden of taxation on the country to pay for his wars, and once said he would have sold London if he could find a buyer, at most half in jest. And on one of those "glorious" military expeditions he got himself taken hostage by Leopold V, Duke of Austria, over ludicrously complex dynastic quarrels that ended up with his being handed over to the Holy Roman Emperor Henry VI.

Henry VI demanded a ransom of 150,000 marks, a huge sum, about twice the annual income of the entire kingdom of England. John got saddled with trying to raise that money to get his brother back, a significant cause of John's extortionate taxation during Richard's absence that is much commented on in the Robin Hood stories without reference to the cause. But we're not letting John off the hook.

He clearly enjoyed the work. And he wasn't doing it all for dear Richard. Indeed, at one point he offered the Holy Roman Emperor an equal sum to turn Richard over to him. And if he had, Richard would probably have disappeared just as John's nephew Arthur came to a mysterious tragic end at John's hands after John succeeded Richard.

You might think, well, murdering a nephew was just par for the course in those days. A rival to the throne vanishes, not safe to say anything about it. But the fact is, John took tendencies that were developing under Richard and made them worse. And his contemporaries, the barons, the knights, the people who fought against John did it not because they wished that government could be different than it always had been, but because John wasn't respecting their traditional liberties and they were determined to get them back. Magna Carta was their way of forcing the king to acknowledge that these rights had always existed and always would.

Stephen Langton: A Hero for Our Times

The story of Magna Carta has villains, most prominently King John. But it also has heroes, both sung and unsung. In the former category is one of the most remarkable figures in English history, honourably buried in Canterbury Cathedral: Stephen Langton, Archbishop of Canterbury from 1207 to his death in 1228. Langton is the man credited with dividing the Bible into chapters we still use today, which would be achievement enough for most men. But his influence and importance go far beyond that.

Initially, he was the focus of a power struggle between Pope Innocent III and King John, who were at loggerheads for years before becoming temporary allies over Magna Carta. Langton was Innocent III's choice in a bitterly contested three-way election for Archbishop of Canterbury. But John refused to acknowledge him, which led to the Pope placing all England under interdict in 1208, forbidding the public celebration of most Catholic sacraments. And when that didn't work, he pronounced John deposed in late 1212 and in January 1213 invited Philip II of France to go and get rid of him. That threat finally brought John to heel, and it was Langton, now safely able to come to England, who pronounced absolution on him. But Langton did so partly on condition that John swear to uphold the liberties granted in his great-grandfather Henry I's Coronation Charter. John, being a vicious weasel, agreed but promptly broke his word. In response

Phil Coates, living history re-enactor, with Stephen Langton's Unknown Charter

Langton in August 1213 assembled a group of leading clerics in Westminster along with some barons, read Henry I's Coronation Charter aloud to them, and persuaded them that John needed to be forced to endorse an updated version. That meeting led directly to Magna Carta.

****

Langton wasn't done. Once Magna Carta was sealed, as noted, John managed to ingratiate himself with the pope and convince him to declare Magna Carta null and void and excommunicate any barons who supported it. But Langton refused to read that sentence of excommunication out. Thus he was suspended, then reinstated on condition that he leave England and not come back until peace was restored. After John and Innocent died, Henry III made peace with the barons, and Philip's son Louis and his armies were driven out of England, allowing Langton to return in 1218. He quickly again became a leading figure in opposition now to misgovernment by Henry, and was instrumental in persuading the barons in 1223 that Henry should be obliged to re-issue Magna Carta yet again.

Thus in a long career, in which Langton was first and foremost a churchman, he stood up for the pope against the king, then for the barons against the pope, always for truth and honour, even at great personal risk. If you are in Canterbury Cathedral it is well worth visiting his tomb, now lodged oddly halfway out of the wall because of later renovations to this part of the church, to pay your respects to the bones of a true hero to whom we all owe a debt of gratitude.

The Battle for Rochester Castle

Magna Carta did not come into existence, nor was it preserved, solely because of giants like Langton. It is important to understand that the English political community rallied time and again to the cause of liberty, the great and the small alike. For instance, at Rochester Castle, a splendidly preserved strongpoint on the river Medway in Kent, in south-east England, that was the scene of a bitter siege in the fall of 1215. Just four months after he agreed to Magna Carta, John had an army on the move from Dover to London to try and undo the Great Charter. But this castle had been entrusted to our old friend Stephen Langton, and he had staffed it with men loyal to the barons who refused to let John's forces cross the Medway.[14]

Some were nobles or knights whose names we know. But there

were crossbowmen, foot-soldiers and others long forgotten without whose support the castle could not have defied the king. And it cannot have been an easy decision given John's well-earned reputation for malice petty and grand.

For instance, when John's men invested the castle on the king's orders they ransacked Rochester Cathedral next door to the castle and, to add insult to injury for Langton, stabled their horses in it. But medieval castles were difficult things to take with the technology of the period. So John's forces resorted to tunneling. They mined under the south-east corner of the keep, shoring up their diggings with timber baulks so the castle walls wouldn't come down prematurely on their heads. John then got his justiciar to send him "40 fat pigs of the kind least good for eating."

The soldiers took the fat of those pigs, greased up the timber, set it on fire, and the corner of the keep came tumbling down. But even then the defenders hung on, defending half of the keep for another five days before starvation rather than brute force drove them out.

John meanwhile erected a memorial to the pigs and a gallows where he said he would hang all of the defenders. But one of his commanders pointed out to him that he might one day, the fortunes of war being such as they are, be captured himself and bitterly regret that precedent. So he only hanged one person.

The siege and its outcome are a reminder that when we talk about the courage it took to uphold liberty we don't just mean the people who wound up with marble effigies in cathedrals. We mean every man, and the women behind him, who stood with sword or bow in hand in defiance of tyranny, in Rochester and on countless other battlefields throughout England. That kind of courage made Magna Carta possible, not just in 1215 but on down through succeeding centuries to our own time. And it is not obsolete today. Nor is Magna Carta, which must be preserved in our hearts as well as in glass cases.

The Star of the Show

Only four "exemplars" of the original 1215 Magna Carta are still in existence. They are not properly speaking "copies"; each one is as authentic and authoritative as any other. Two are in the British Library, one in Lincoln Cathedral and one at Salisbury Cathedral where it was proudly on display for the 800th anniversary in 2015. It's the best preserved one, in an exceptionally fine hand, apparently using superior ink, and is believed to have been brought there by Elias of Durham or Dereham, another remarkable figure from that period, a go-to guy who was given the task of getting Salisbury Cathedral built and got it done in just 38 years, quite a feat considering they had no power tools.

Elias was also responsible for distributing 10 of the original exemplars of Magna Carta. We're not sure quite how many were made in total. There were supposed to be 39 or 40, one for every county. But King John, who was plotting to break his word before the wax on the seal had even hardened, wasn't all that keen on making sure copies were distributed.

The Salisbury Magna Carta, ready for its close-up

Neither to be sure were some of the barons, often rough and ready military men. But the Church was very concerned, partly because Magna Carta among other things guarantees the liberties of the Church, ensuring that it will not be a creature of the state. And so Elias made sure his own cathedral had a fine copy, to be consulted and appealed to down through the years. And it is still there, preserved and honoured as part of the legacy of freedom of thought in the English-speaking world.

The Battle for Dover Castle

Another castle important to the story is the magnificent, and wonderfully refurbished, Dover Castle overlooking the famous White Cliffs. Dover isn't just the largest castle in England. It's been a vital strong point from pre-Roman times, dubbed "The Key to England". There's an iron-age hillfort, on which the Romans built. As soon as the Normans got here they knew they better put a castle up, and the fortifications were added to and modified down through the years, including in Napoleonic times when cannons were installed and some of the medieval stone work was removed to give a better field of fire. As late as World War II, it was in service; Admiral Sir Bertram Ramsay directed the evacuation from Dunkirk from tunnels constructed during the Napoleonic Wars.

One of the curious incidents in the fighting for Magna Carta occurred at Dover Castle when, in 1216 and again in 1217, Prince Louis, son of King Philip II of France, besieged it. Its central keep, built by Henry II, was the main target of Louis's forces but it was just too strong for them to take.

It might seem curious that Louis was making war in England in the first place, or that the factions quarreling over Magna Carta should not have composed their differences long enough to make common cause against him. Instead some of the barons invited him to come in and become king of England in place of the tyrannical John, whom the Pope had earlier authorized Philip to depose.

To understand why inviting Louis over was not a spectacular act of disloyalty on the part of English nobles, it's important to remember that the Anglo-Norman ruling class had come over with William the Conqueror from France in 1066. They did not think of "England" and "France" as inherently separate entities, let alone inherently opposed ones as they would come to seem from the 14th century on through the late 19th. Many English lords still had land in France, including King John, who was the Duke of Normandy and Count of Anjou among other French titles. What's more, these kings of England, as Norman

Davies reminds us in his book *The Isles*, didn't speak a word of English. Properly we ought to call them Henri Deux, Jean Sans-Terre, and Edouard Premier. John may have been the first English king to be born and die in England since Harold Godwinson.[15] But not until Edward III do you have a king who can speak comfortably to his subjects in their own language. And not until Henry V in the 15th century are royal proclamations made in English.

Does that mean that but for the fortunes of battle, the thickness of the walls at Dover, the determination of the defenders and the energetic leadership of Henry III's forces by the aged William Marshal, Magna Carta might be a footnote and England might have become part of the continent? No. Political culture runs deeper than that, and a key reason Louis didn't become king of England is Marshal's success, after John died, in persuading the new boy king Henry III to re-issue Magna Carta and promise he would respect the liberties his father had scorned and trampled underfoot.

Kings may come and go but political culture is enduring and no one could become king of England and hold the throne who did not respect the rights of his subjects. To say so is not to declare that Henry III had either the intention to respect their liberties or the force of character to uphold any resolve he might form. It is to say that misrule on John's or even Henry's scale dependably roused the effective opposition of the English.

Simon de Montfort: A Hero for Parliament

England's historic Evesham Abbey, which had stood for some eight centuries by the time Henry VIII dissolved the monasteries and most of its buildings were knocked down, marks the spot where parts of Simon de Montfort, Earl of Leicester, are buried. The commemorative plaque marking the 700th anniversary of his death in the battle of Evesham on August 4, 1265 describes him as "pioneer of representative government." It is an accolade he thoroughly deserves.

Simon led baronial opposition to and two full-scale revolts against Bad King John's son Henry III, a feckless monarch with most of his father's minor failings but without the ruthless cunning and energy that made John a truly dangerous man. Henry was always in debt, spending money he didn't have, a weak hand on the tiller of state. He did establish London's first zoo; it had a rhinoceros, a polar bear, it had lions, and visitors were invited to bring a dog or cat to feed to the lions, which would certainly have made Henry an unpopular monarch had he tried that today. What made him an unpopular monarch back then was that he was an ineffective ruler and an extravagant spender.

Remonstrances proved to be of no avail; efforts to impose formal limits on Henry's power met with slippery evasion; and finally Simon led the Second Baronial War in 1264. And unlike the petty dynastic quarrels that disfigure the history of so many nations, this struggle was over important principles. And unlike the sorry history of so many parts of our troubled planet, it ended with a lasting victory for justice and human rights if not for many of the actual rebels.

In the course of this revolt, Montfort captured the king and his son, the future Edward I. And then he did two things that make him a great man.

After capturing the king and his heir, Simon had a problem. How could he cloak his action, effectively taking over the kingdom, with the mantle of legitimate authority, both against the king and against his fellow rebel barons, some of whom might aspire to supreme power themselves? In many parts of the world the answer would have been intimidation: Stick the king's head on a post, slaughter your enemies in heaps, or pile up a big pyramid of skulls.

In England you did it by basing your claim to power on the rights of the common man. So Simon took Henry III to Westminster Abbey, made him re-issue Magna Carta before God and man, and then summoned a parliament, a council of the realm. Such gatherings had been held in various informal ways going back to Saxon times, for instance to try to settle the question of who became King on the death of Edward the Confessor. But as noted above, such bodies had no corporate existence, no rules of procedure, no institutional independence, no official capacity to convene themselves in times of crisis. They were important but informal advisory councils. And in the original Magna Carta and under the 1258 "Provisions of Oxford" through which his unhappy nobles had tried to bind Henry III, ad hoc councils of barons were established with improvised mixed executive and legislative power. But Henry's reign saw increasing if irregular sessions of "parliaments" that included some representation by the rural gentry as well as great nobles.

****

Under Montfort the nature of Parliament changed permanently because he brought in a key innovation: He invited in the common people as full participants able to comment on general matters of governance. He summoned two knights from every county, and for the first time included the towns and cities, in the form of two burgesses from every major town except the Cinq Ports who got four. And they genuinely seem to have been freely chosen by local citizens. As Daniel Hannan notes in *Inventing Freedom*, "Extraordinarily – and uniquely in Europe at that time – he [Montfort] asked that these representatives be directly elected, and as far as we can tell, the vote was open to every freeholder: it wasn't until two hundred years later that a tax threshold was imposed, and the franchise thereby restricted."[16]

Evesham Abbey

It was an extraordinary decision with extraordinary consequences. Simon himself came to a bad end. Prince Edward escaped, rallied an army including many nobles unhappy with growing popular influence, and defeated Montfort at Evesham where he was killed and dismembered. Roger Mortimer, who actually killed him, reportedly draped his testicles round his severed head and sent the resulting object to Mortimer's own evidently rather gruesome wife as a gift, while Montfort's hands and feet were also sent to various enemies. The remaining pieces were interred under the altar at Evesham until Henry VIII had them dug up and reburied under a random tree.

In many parts of the world it would have been the end of Montfort's reforms as well. But not in England, where his broadening of Parliament had made a strong impression on the common people. Instead, after Edward became king in 1272, a masterful man, the hated "Longshanks" of Braveheart, he regularly convened parliaments and also summoned two knights from every county and two burgesses from every major town. As the king himself put it, possibly through clenched teeth, "what touches all shall be decided by all".[17]

Once the common people were brought in, they could not again be excluded because in England, the legitimacy of government depended, as it always had, upon protecting the rights of the common man. And Edward could no more govern, including taxing, without popular consent than Henry III, John or anyone else. Indeed, Edward personally confirmed Magna Carta no fewer than 11 times in the course of his reign. It was fundamental law, to the point that it was expressly declared that any statute contrary to it was null and void. And it was fundamental because it came from the people and protected their rights.

To be sure, Simon de Montfort was not a flawless character. Among his failings there was a streak of vicious anti-Semitism in his revolt and in his popular appeal. His rights of the common man tragically failed to include the Jews, who were in fact banished from England under Edward I in 1290.[18] But for all that, he did help Englishmen turn the institutionally vague promise in the original Magna Carta of no taxation without the general consent of the kingdom, with which they had fumbled through much of the 13th century, into far stronger and sharper form by bringing the common people into the parliaments of England from which they were never again displaced. Instead they continued to gain in power and influence, establishing control of their own affairs and of the power of the purse by the very early 15th century. For that Simon de Montfort is celebrated at Evesham not because he was an important noble but because he was a pioneer of representative government. And indeed he was.

Liberty for the Common Man

One curious misunderstanding that frequently arises about Magna Carta, despite Montfort's parliament and other such evidence, is that it was somehow an elite deal. In keeping with the prevalent conviction that history is an unbroken progression from the bad old days to the magnificent present,[19] people say that while Magna Carta contained some good ideas about political order in embryonic form, it took centuries to apply the concept of rights to the common person.

One characteristic statement holds that "During the Middle Ages, the powers of political rulers in relation to some classes of subjects came to be limited by legal agreements, the most prominent example being Magna Carta. But these were merely accidental results of power struggles among various groups and classes. The key turn in constitutional history comes with the development by John Locke and others of a natural law theory including inalienable personal rights."[20] A website devoted to British history and culture asserted on the 800th anniversary of the first sealing of Magna Carta that "The text of the 'Great Charter', granted by the King at Runnymede on June 15 1215, fails to even mention the notion of universal rights – in reality, it is a document concerned with the rights of an elite."[21] And even Carolyn Harris's splendid *Magna Carta and its Gifts to Canada* asserts that "Modern interpretations of Magna Carta are not informed by the intentions of thirteenth-century rebel barons but by seventeenth-century jurists – most notably, Sir Edward Coke".[22]

This notion is incompatible with the text itself or the subsequent political development of England. Magna Carta may not have used the language of 20th-century human rights bureaucrats. But the final clause of the 1215 original says "It is accordingly our wish and command that the English Church shall be free, and that men in our kingdom shall have and keep all these liberties, rights, and concessions, well and peaceably in their fulness and entirety for them and their heirs, of us and our heirs, in all things and all places for ever."

Not nobles. Not prelates. Not rich and powerful men. Simply men. Indeed in the original Latin it says *homines*, which designates people generally rather than specifically male persons, which would be *viri*.

As the great jurist and statesman Edward Coke would note pointedly four centuries later, brandishing the Great Charter against

Stuart pretensions to absolute rule, Henry III's confirmation of Magna Carta in 1225 greeted nobles, clerics, minor officials "and other our faithful Subjects", saying "Know Ye, that We, unto the honour of Almighty God, and for the salvation of the souls of our Progenitors and Successors Kings of England, to the advancement of Holy Church and amendment of our Realm, of our meer and free will, have given and granted to all Archbishops, Bishops, Abbots, Priors, Earls, Barons, and to all Freemen of this our Realm, these Liberties following, to be kept in our Kingdom of England for ever."[23] And, Coke added, "These words (*omnibus liberis hominibus regni* [all Freemen of our Realm]) doe include all persons Ecclesiasticall and temporall and temporal incorporate politique or naturall, nay they extend also to villeines [serfs], for they are accounted free against all men saving against the Lords."[24] And as Geoffrey Hindley observes, in August 1234, Henry III issued royal letters "asserting that the Charters [Magna Carta and the Charter of the Forest] are granted to both great and small and to all men."[25]

That is why from the time of Edward I, before the end of the 13th century, it was decreed that Magna Carta should be read aloud in all the cathedrals twice a year, in the vernacular, so that everybody would know what it said, even humble folk who could not read. Indeed, late in his reign it was being read aloud four times a year in county courts as well. Of course in the cathedral readings it was sometimes being translated on the fly by clerics who might occasionally have botched what they were saying. But the fact is that there was a deliberate legislative enactment that it should be made available to the general populace in a form they could understand so that everybody, all free men, would know what their rights were.

Magna Carta guaranteed everyone's rights from the beginning, and it meant exactly what it said from the beginning. And while it is true that the protective circle of rights it drew was not always drawn broadly enough, and it sometimes excluded people with tragic consequences, the intention from the beginning was that the phrase "homo liber" meant everybody.

That is why the admission of the common people to Parliament, better to secure those liberties, could never be reversed. Indeed, no one ever seriously suggested trying. Which contrasts dramatically with the history of virtually any other nation even in continental Europe, where popular assemblies were unknown, intermittent or eventually suppressed and had minimal impact on public policy.

Odiham Castle

Odiham Castle, west of London, has been a ruin for many centuries now. But it was a popular and in some ways quite an important spot in its day.

It was originally constructed by King John, starting in 1207, as a strong point but also as a hunting lodge. It sits on very marshy ground. Even the raised earth on which the remains stand today is an artificial mound built by press-gang peasants. The boggy surroundings and cunning construction made Odiham very easy to defend with a fairly small group. It was besieged by Prince Louis in 1216, and held out for two weeks. When the garrison finally surrendered the French were amazed to find there were just 13 men inside.

It was also from Odiham that John rode to Runnymede to seal

Magna Carta, and he came back there afterward. A copy of Magna Carta was recently found in Rouen in French that was made in Odiham on John's orders within two weeks of the sealing. Copies were made in French because that was the language of most of the administration of Norman England even though the original Magna Carta was in Latin and most of the populace spoke Middle English at that time. And while John didn't much like Magna Carta he was supposed to send out copies and he did at least send out a few before he got the Pope to annul it.

Later, under Henry III, Odiham was given to Henry's then-widowed sister Eleanor, who eventually married Simon de Montfort without Henry's permission, one among many points of contention between Montfort and the king. And it was from Odiham that Montfort and his eldest son Henry rode out to their last battle at Evesham where they were both killed by Edward, later Edward I.

Odiham Castle later fell into disrepair because the ground wasn't suitable for building the larger, more elaborate castle characteristic of the 14th and 15th centuries. But it is noteworthy today not just for its historic importance and ambiance but as a standing warning to people in England and elsewhere that institutions like buildings can crumble into ruins if they're not actively maintained by people who care deeply about why they're here and what they're for.

The work of Langton, Montfort, William Marshal and countless others in codifying and preserving liberty under law have lasted down through the centuries because great and small alike rallied to the principles of freedom and its institutional defenses when they were threatened. If we cease to do so, they too will crumble into quaint historical relics unsuitable for inhabitation.

Part II

The Triumph of Liberty

Westminster Abbey has stood in the heart of London through almost every important event in British history that you've ever heard of. It was founded by the last reigning Saxon king, Edward the Confessor, in 1065 though of course much of the most ornate work is later medieval. But this cathedral was here when Magna Carta was sealed. It was here during the English Civil War, it was here during the American Revolution, it was here during the Blitz.

Westminster has particular relevance to our story for two reasons. First, when Simon de Montfort, leader of a baronial revolt, captured King Henry III and his son Edward in 1265, he brought the king here and forced him to re-issue Magna Carta before God and man.

Secondly, as the British Parliament developed and the House of Commons established its own identity, it was regarded at first as the poor cousin branch, and lacking a formal meeting place like the Lords, it gathered wherever its members could put their muddy feet, including sometimes at Westminster Abbey.

What mattered much more than where they were meeting was the fact that they were meeting. They continued to meet and they eventually became as permanent and dignified a part of the British system as Westminster Abbey.

Here comes Parliament

The development of Parliament in the later Middle Ages is as critical as it is unusual. Where such institutions were fading out on the continent, in England Parliament and particularly the House of Commons went from strength to strength.

The first critical step came under Edward I in 1297 when the king, broke as usual, assented to a specific statute, *De Tallagio non Concedendo*, declaring that the king could not raise money without parliamentary assent. When the American revolutionaries made "No taxation without representation" a rallying cry in 1776 it was not a new principle and they did not imagine for a moment that it was. They were not innovating and were not trying to. Instead they were asserting rights already half a millennium old, marching in the footsteps of those who had defended them against all challengers for 500 years.

Of course Edward I had his own revenues as a great noble, and some traditional prerogatives that furnished money. Budgeting in those days was a patchwork of traditional measures, desperate expedients[26] and determined evasion by the English of levies they considered unfair. Among other things the national budget was still calculated using Roman numerals and a chequered cloth to simply the mind-boggling task of multiplying and dividing in that system, which is why the British finance minister is the "Chancellor of the Exchequer" to this day. But Edward could neither impose new forms of taxation, increase existing ones, or collect those that required a fresh parliamentary grant, without securing one.

The crucial practical problem, which was to arise repeatedly over the next 500 years and indeed beyond, was how exactly to give institutional form and solidity to the basic guarantee that taxes could not be levied without, as the original Magna Carta had put it, the "general consent" of the realm. *De tallagio* itself, and the parliaments including commoners first summoned by Montfort, were a partial answer. But the question of how exactly Parliament must function to make those guarantees a reality still had to be answered in a sensible and binding way. And it was, with remarkable swiftness. Again, the notion that people did not take the rights of the commoners seriously early on, that Magna Carta was really only for the high and mighty, is impossible to reconcile with what happened within a century and a half of its initial sealing.

To begin with, while Montfort's and Edward's parliaments met as one single chamber, the representatives of the towns and shires had begun meeting separately as a corporate body by 1346. Revealingly, we

Medieval Parliament under Edward

don't know exactly when or how it began to happen. Probably it had its roots in informal caucuses of these "common, base and popular" representatives before joint sessions with the high and mighty nobles and clergy. But those caucuses of knights and burgesses developed such a strong sense of identity and purpose, and maintained such cohesion in the face of pressure from their supposed betters, that they soon constituted a separate chamber with its own rights and privileges.

The importance of that development cannot be overstated. Despite being regarded as the poor cousins, at least socially, to the point that they lacked their own dedicated meeting place and nobody bothered to record exactly when they started holding formal separate sessions, the Commons swiftly acquired and jealously guarded control of their own affairs including, by 1376, the critical step of electing their own Speaker.

It may seem curious to casual observers of parliaments ancient or modern that the title of "Speaker" is bestowed on the one member who does not speak in debates. But his or her role is far more important: to speak as the sole voice of a united House in dealing with the other branches. The Speaker determines when the House sits and when it rises; how and when debates and votes shall proceed; the Speaker counts the votes and the Speaker and only the Speaker says what the House has decided.

Without these powers the Commons would have been a mere appendage of the monarchy. As Joseph Stalin once observed with cynical acuity, it doesn't matter who votes, it matters who counts the votes. If the result of parliamentary debates was that the king did so, or could ignore what really happened by persuading a supine faction to endorse his agenda, the Commons would be powerless. But he did not and could not, at any point in English history.[27]

Instead, the House very quickly asserted its authority over both monarch and Lords. In 1399 Edward III's grandson Richard II, son of Edward "the Black Prince", was deposed by the general consent of all classes for refusing to accept limits on his power. He tampered with records of parliamentary debates and infamously claimed "the law is in my mouth", that is, that he could legislate by mere royal proclamation.

And those who deposed him, like those who deposed Edward II in 1327, cited Magna Carta in justifying their rebellion.

****

Henry of Bolingbroke, grandson of Edward III by his third son John of Gaunt,[28] then claimed the throne as Henry IV. But to secure his claim, he needed the backing of Parliament. And when he sought it, it was offered with a singularly important condition attached.

Parliamentarians told the man who would be king that, in the past, monarchs had been wont to summon Parliaments, hear their grievances and then ask for money. But once their revenue requests were satisfied, they quickly lost interest in their subjects' concerns. So, Henry was told, if he wished to be king he must promise that from now on, he would answer petitions and grievances before being granted money. In short, the modern system of royal assent to bills as a condition of "supply" was created in the late Middle Ages.

Another key step occurred just seven years later, when the Commons confronted the Lords over a money bill, insisting that they had primacy, and Henry IV confirmed the Lords' acquiescence, saying Parliament could confer in his absence "always provided that neither the Lords... nor the Commons... shall make any report to our said Lord the King of any grant made by the Commons and assented to by the Lords, or of the discussions in connection with the said grant, until the same Lords and Commons are of one mind and accord in this matter, and then... by the mouth of the Speaker of the said Commons ..."[29]

Note the wording "made by the Commons and assented to by the Lords" and that the final report of it shall come from the House Speaker. To this day, of course, money bills must originate in the lower House in Canada, Britain and the United States.

In 1414 yet another critical refinement in the system of passing money bills was made when the Commons forced the new king, Henry V, to agree that he could accept or reject but not alter Commons bills and, particularly, that he not presume to change their text after MPs, having granted money in return for his acceptance of them, had gone home.

In short, the fundamental structure of the modern power of the purse was in place before Agincourt. It would be challenged repeatedly, sometimes dangerously, over the next three hundred years. But when it was, defenders of liberty and the principle of no taxation without representation sought always to preserve and refine this essentially medieval system, not create some new and marvelous abstraction.

Parliament and Magna Carta

This growing power of Parliament happened in the shadow of Magna Carta explicitly as well as implicitly. Under both Edward I and Edward III it was expressly enacted that any statute contrary to Magna Carta was null and void, even if passed using correct procedure and receiving royal assent. Edward I had reissued Magna Carta repeatedly including in 1297 and again in 1300. But after that it was deliberately incorporated into statute law though without being reduced to a simple statute capable of amendment rather than mere clarification or enforcement by acts of Parliament. Like the American Constitution nearly half a millennium later, it stood above statute law, limiting what Parliament as well as the King could do.

Thus we see a series of laws, the "Six Statutes," passed under

Edward III between 1331 and 1369 that seek to clarify the meaning of various parts of Magna Carta. In the third of these, in 1354, the cherished phrase "due process of law" is introduced with respect to "lawful judgement of his peers or the law of the land". And, revealingly, the crucial phrase "free man" was defined as "no man, of whatever estate or condition he may be". If, as some scholars maintain, it was not the intention of barons and clerics in 1215 to secure the rights of ordinary people, it is surely remarkable, even inexplicable, that such a measure would be passed within 150 years during which Magna Carta continued to be affirmed by monarchs dozens of times, including by Henry VI in 1423, and frequently read as the first item of parliamentary business.

The position of Magna Carta above statute law is crucial to understanding what had evolved in England by the end of the Middle Ages. Parliament was not an institution of unchecked majority rule in place of unchecked executive rule. It had no power whatsoever to override the traditional rights of Englishmen, on its own or in partnership with the monarch and his advisors. There was no point in Kings trying to coopt, bribe or intimidate Parliament into giving them what John had tried to take by force.

Thus when we speak of Parliament's "growing power" we mean its growing power to restrain the executive branch in the name of traditional liberties. But since any statute contrary to Magna Carta was null and void it had no power to infringe those liberties in any way for any reason. And thus, again, the American Constitution was not an attempt to break with the past but to give fresh and even more solid institutional form to the ancient British constitution believed, with good reason, to be under threat in the 18th century.[30]

The Inns of Court

Parliament did not grow up in a vacuum, of course. If it had, it would not have survived and prevailed. Instead, it grew from the rich soil of the common law and the rights of Englishmen.

Historians tend to present the rising power of the English Parliament as a natural consequence of the financial needs of English monarchs. One typical account, in Norman Davies' compelling *The Isles*, says "By the end of 1340, however, Edouard III was bankrupt. He had debts to the tune of £300,000 – a sum equal to perhaps ten times his annual income. He could not return from the Continent until he had sold part of the crown jewels to pay the troops. Yet this early financial crisis had long-term benefits. It forced him to match his ambitions to his means; and it encouraged the ever closer partnership of King and Parliament that was to become the hallmark of English governance.... As early as 1338, in the Walton Ordinances, provision had been made to make regular financial estimates, 'to enquire into the extent of the King's debts and liabilities and to estimate the revenue necessary to meet them' – in other words to prepare a budget. One of the few such rudimentary financial exercises to leave documentary evidence dates from a slightly later decade..."[31]

It all sounds so logical and plausible. But contrast it with the equally smooth and convincing account in Nobel economics laureate Douglass North and Robert Paul Thomas's *The Rise of the Western World* of the French monarchy's financial crisis less than a century later. As his military fortunes revived at the end of the Hundred Years War, they blithely note, King Charles VII "while successful in eliminating close competitors for his throne, was at the same time still in a position to raise substantial sums from his subjects in order to rid the countryside of the scourging effects of military brigands. Thus Charles obtained a monopoly of protection in France. Increasingly in the 1430s the king treated *Aides*, like the *Gabelle*, as his prerogative, a tax to be levied without consent. The assembly at Orleans in 1439, proved to be the last national assembly to approve the *Taille*. While Charles VII did appeal for funds from local assemblies as late as 1451, the king's control over taxing power had actually become complete after 1439. The Estates General had surrendered control over taxing power in the process of providing Charles VII with the finances to maintain an army that would defend the borders and eliminate the marauders from within."[32]

****

Now either process makes sense in isolation. But the great puzzle is why such similar fiscal problems should have driven English monarchs into ever deeper reliance on popular assemblies while enabling French monarchs to dispense with them, to say nothing of developments elsewhere like Russia, where practically the first act of Ivan III after throwing off the Mongol yoke was to impose his own, conquering the Republic of Novgorod, crushing its *veche* or popular assembly and carrying off its assembly bell in triumph to Moscow.

By 1527 the president of the highest French court expressly told François I "we do not wish to dispute or minimize your power; that would be sacrilege, and we know very well that you are above the laws"[33] while Jean Bodin, a leading political theorist, member of the Paris Parlement and professor of law could write in the 16th century "When edicts are ratified by Estates or Parlements, it is for the purpose of securing obedience to them, and not because otherwise a sovereign prince could not validly make law".[34] And so it proved; no French Estates General even met between 1614 and the French Revolution.

Something is different in England. And while the development of Parliament helps to express, refine and strengthen the difference, it also depends vitally upon it. The principles of liberty, in an orderly, functioning, popularly accessible legal system, permeated British public institutions from such early times that their origins are lost to history. For instance the Inns of Court including Lincoln's Inn, a characteristically British institution. Law students had been studying there from time immemorial when Edward Coke became Speaker of the House of Commons, and that was under Elizabeth I in 1593.

Nobody quite knows how the Inns of Court got started but by Coke's day some of the finest legal minds in England, men with important legal responsibilities, members of Parliament, came and taught there for free. Why? Because it was bred in the bone that the rule of law was important. Not just what the law said, but that the law as written was applied, and was applied fairly.

The law in Coke's days wouldn't have met contemporary standards in many respects. Coke himself boasted that the laws of England did not permit torture but he knew perfectly well that the king's prerogative did. As attorney general, he prosecuted cases where torture had been used. In Coke's day, defendants couldn't call witnesses. And in nearby Lincoln's Inn Fields, executions were carried out using methods that we today would consider inappropriate. But that doesn't mean people in Coke's day were either fools or hypocrites.

Their devotion to the rule of law, to improving it, in theory and in practice, to assuring that it was applied to everyone from commoners up to the monarch, tireless efforts over the centuries to make it a reality are why we have the legal systems that we have and cherish today.[35]

History tends to focus on "high politics" which leave a larger footprint and are easier to summarize. But the slow steady resistance of an alert political class to pernicious innovations, and the tendency of the public to rally to traditional freedoms if events come to a crisis, have a critical background influence on the preservation of liberty in times of particular peril.

King Henry the Dangerous

One of these occurred in the Renaissance, under Henry VIII. The end of the Middle Ages saw the rise of absolutism throughout Europe and even England faced a new dynasty, the Tudors, with large ambitions not just in the world but in England's political system.

The last Tudor, Elizabeth I, was a woman of nice judgement and mostly decent instincts, fondly remembered as "Gloriana" or "Good Queen Bess" depending on your social station. But her father Henry VIII, an outsized polymath credited among other things with writing "Greensleeves", was not just a threat to his various wives. Though not the worst king in English history, he was probably the most dangerous to liberty since King John. But English liberty had cultural and institutional reserves of strength absent in France, Spain or anywhere else except perhaps Scandinavia.

Throughout Europe, the feudal nobility was in decline. And in Spain and France, as in a lesser way in smaller polities including Prussia, there seemed to be no effective counterweight to the rising national state headed by a king or emperor. It is France, not England, that is the typical case here.

The decline of the nobility had complex causes, partly intellectual and partly economic, including the more effective centralized bureaucracy made possible by the printing press. But the immediate cause was the invention of gunpowder cannons, which rendered feudal castles vulnerable to quick attack rather than prolonged and exhausting siege. And whatever its causes, it revealed the lack of "civil society" of the English sort.

In past centuries the nobility had so thoroughly dominated kings and princes that it had not needed anything a resembling partnership with the common people or lesser gentry. By the 16th century, it was far too late to develop one.

The one major exception was England, where you had Parliament, with its House of Commons grounded in local gentry and burgesses drawn from the ordinary people, and the rights of Magna Carta to which the people and their representatives were devoted. And the vital importance of this structure, and Churchill's "Constitution opposition," is dramatically underlined at a critical moment in 1539. Henry VIII, who sometimes lost parliamentary votes on minor matters but four years earlier had told a leading parliamentarian bluntly "Get my Bill passed by to-morrow, or else to-morrow this head of yours will be off!", ordered Parliament to pass a Statute of Proclamations saying his decrees had the force of law.

It was precisely the claim for which Richard II had been deposed in 1399. To adopt it meant the end of any check on royal power. But to refuse could mean sudden bloody death. So Parliament again found a characteristically English way of bending their knee to the king while kicking him hard in the backside.

Richard II

MPs adopted an alternative bill that supposedly granted his wish but specifically exempted the "'inheritances, lawful possessions, offices, liberties, privileges, franchises, goods, or chattels' of subjects, and forbade the infringement of any 'acts, common laws.... [or] lawful and laudable customs' of the realm."[36] In short, now you see it, now you don't, Hank. And thus Henry was obliged to act through Parliament even when dispatching wives, stealing monasteries and making himself Pope of England.

Henry was a masterful man, intolerant of opposition, capable of great boldness in pursuit of great designs and dangerous to those around him both male and female. He was able to have Thomas More executed for opposing his break with Rome despite More's invocation of Magna Carta's protection for the freedom of the Church.[37] But he could not do any of it without the support of Parliament.

The Importance of Religious Freedom

There is a candle on the floor of Canterbury Cathedral that marks the very spot where the remains of St. Thomas Becket are not buried. And that's important to our story in two ways. Becket was the Archbishop of Canterbury who was famously murdered on the orders or at least because of the careless words of King Henry II in 1170.[38] He had been the king's right-hand man. Henry had him appointed Archbishop of Canterbury and it apparently didn't occur to him that a man who was a faithful servant of the Crown in a royal post might become a faithful servant of the Church in an ecclesiastical post. But so it proved. Becket upheld the rights of the Church against the monarch, insisting that England was a land in which the Church did not need to aspire to rule the state in order to avoid being enslaved by it.

The murder shocked the nation. And Henry didn't get away with it. Four years later he was forced to admit to it, to appear in the cathedral mute in sackcloth, and to prostrate himself naked on the floor while monks whipped him. Becket's bones were interred in the cathedral. They were moved to the spot where the candle now is 50 years after his death in 1220 and it quickly became a shrine. Becket was canonized, and pilgrims flocked to the shrine until 1538 when, as part of the dissolution of the monasteries, Henry VIII had the shrine and the bones themselves destroyed.

Henry had just broken with Rome and made himself effectively the English Pope, so that he could divorce his wife Catherine of Aragon and marry his mistress Anne Boleyn. And he had his own former Lord High Chancellor and trusted friend Thomas More executed for opposing him on this issue. So the last thing he wanted was people remembering a man who was martyred for standing up for the Church against the Crown and succeeding despite losing his life. Henry wanted to rule the Church, he wanted the Church lands and he got them. But in England he couldn't do these remarkable extravagant things and didn't dare try without the support of Parliament. Even such an outsized figure, in an era of outsized rulers, could not crush the liberties of the English the way he did manage to crush the bones of Thomas Becket.

****

England was not free of religious controversy after Henry's break with Rome. On the contrary, religion was the backdrop to a series of upheavals under Bloody Mary and later the Stuarts, suspected of wishing to re-impose Catholicism as well as inflict novel tyranny on England. These controversies had a particularly sharp edge because while England had of course been Catholic since the earliest evangelization of the Saxons in the 6th and 7th centuries, the English had always balanced their religious obligations to the pope with a lively, determined and sometimes ingenious refusal to acknowledge his political authority.

Even John, despite his shady dealings with Innocent III around Magna Carta, was at one time admired to a limited degree precisely for refusing to bend the royal knee to Rome. And this habit was firmly maintained from William the Conqueror on down, in a typically English way.

During one memorable confrontation under Edward III, the king basically told the pope he couldn't accede to papal demands that undermined Parliament, while Parliament told the pope they couldn't accede to papal demands that undermined the king, and so His Holiness could in effect go jump in the Tiber.

Under Richard II it was made an offence to bring papal bulls into England as a revision to the Statute of Praemunire passed by Parliament in 1353 due to that previous confrontation. That 1353 statute made it a major offence to undermine the sovereignty of England by word or deed and created the weighty writ of praemunire against anyone who did so, on behalf of the pope or anyone else.[39]

Thus we see that even in matters of church and state the assertion of the inalienable rights of Englishmen, expressed through Parliament, set the island kingdom sharply apart even when it did share Catholicism with continental regimes. At all times, even in these matters, vital questions of state, of liberty and of law remained in the hands of elected representatives who might sometimes bend but never broke.

Even at the critical point in 1539, perhaps most dangerous moment in English history since 1215, for the rights of Englishmen, parliamentarians found their courage, confident in the support of the community, stood on the rights enshrined in Magna Carta and the institutions that protected them, and safeguarded freedom for future generations.

Edward Coke: A Hero for Magna Carta

Henry's daughter Elizabeth, lauded by the mighty as "Gloriana" and by the commoners as "Good Queen Bess," had too much sense and decency to provoke a confrontation over the fundamental rights of the English. But when she died without heirs, the throne passed to the autocratic Scottish Stuart dynasty, into which Henry VII had married his daughter Margaret, Henry VIII's older sister, and the Stuarts were determined if often devious absolutists. Their ambitions provoked crises, a civil war and the beheading of a king, more maneuverings and the ousting of another king in the Glorious Revolution. But it all might have turned out very differently without the appearance of another remarkable hero of liberty, Sir Edward Coke.

In the charming, sadly neglected 14th century church of St. Mary's in Tittleshall Norfolk, in the Coke family section, sits a monument to Coke (pronounced "Cook"), one of the greatest men in English history and in the struggle for liberty. He was at various times Solicitor General, Speaker of the House of Commons, Attorney General, Chief Justice of the Court of Common Pleas (the top civil court), Chief Justice of the Court of King's Bench (the top criminal court), Member of Parliament, political prisoner, and again Member of Parliament. And throughout it all he upheld the rights of Englishmen, often needing great courage to do it.

As Speaker of the House of Commons, he lectured Queen Elizabeth on MPs' privilege of free speech. As Chief Justice of the civil court, he openly defied Elizabeth's successor, the paradoxical James I, including in one memorable instance that furnished a shining example to posterity. England had church courts in those days, and James had created an ecclesiastical Court of High Commission with nearly unlimited power that required an oath to answer all questions that might be asked, a sweeping aside of due process, probable cause, protection against self-incrimination and so on.

Coke repeatedly issued writs denying the Court of High Commission jurisdiction over any cases involving secular as well as religious questions. Finally James summoned the various judges before him in a session that rapidly degenerated into sullen silence. A second session went even worse, with James asserting a royal prerogative to settle cases himself. Coke confronted him, saying the common law must prevail. When James said he would always protect the common law Coke retorted to the effect (various accounts of this matter exist) that the common law protected the king not the other way around.

James, who was prone to hysteria, succumbed on this occasion, shrieking "A treasonous speech!" Coke was ultimately forced to go down on his knees and beg forgiveness along with his supporters at court. James did forgive him, and left to go hunting. And Coke went right back to issuing writs of prohibition against the High Commission.

James I

His actions showed extraordinary courage as well as devotion to principle. And they so annoyed the king that James kicked him upstairs to Chief Justice of the top criminal court. And there, again, Coke was instrumental in obstructing the king's efforts to usurp power. At one point he got a group of judges to send a letter to the king telling him his use of the *in commendam* writ to transfer ecclesiastical property was illegal and hence the courts would ignore it. James furiously summoned the judges, berated and patronised them and tore up their letter. The other judges threw themselves on their knees and begged forgiveness. Coke refused, saying "When the case happens I shall do that which shall be fit for a judge to do". James blew his stack, suspended him from the privy council, and fired him as Chief Justice of King's Bench, to general outrage, ordered him to rewrite his famous *Reports* on the proceedings of English courts, and had various court lackeys accuse him of financial irregularities.

Coke didn't back down. Instead he got himself elected to Parliament with the unwise support of the king, who thought he had now brought him to heel. Quite the reverse. Coke immediately became a leading parliamentary opponent of the king's military policies and fiscal demands.

James was a cunning man capable of great folly, or possibly a foolish man capable of great cunning, dubbed by his exceptionally wily contemporary Henri IV of France "the wisest fool in Christendom". He never liked or understood the English system, scolding his very first English parliament that in Edinburgh its tame Scottish equivalent listened to him "not only as a king but as a counselor. Contrary, here, nothing but curiosity from morning to evening to find fault with my propositions. There, all things warranted that came from me. Here, all things suspected!" [40] But though firmly persuaded of the divine right of kings, and contemptuously impatient with the English Parliament, James largely avoided confrontations by avoiding expensive wars.

After his first English Parliament ended in 1611 James managed for 10 years without a parliamentary subsidy and for seven without summoning a Parliament at all, after the brief "addled Parliament" of 1614. That Parliament refused his requests and quarreled with him, prompting his irritated observation that he was "amazed that his ancestors should have allowed such an institution to come into existence" and he plainly intended to allow it to fade into history. But a decade was, as one observer put it, "a long time to live, like a shellfish, on his own moisture" and by 1621 James, too shrewd to try to extort major subsidies without popular sanction, had no choice.

The result was a very stormy session. James bluntly ordered the Speaker of the Commons "to acquaint that house with our pleasure, that none therein shall presume to meddle with anything concerning our government or mysteries of state," threatened to punish MPs for what they might say during debate, and haughtily declared "We cannot allow of the stile, calling it [free speech in Parliament] your antient and undoubted right and inheritance; but could rather have wished that ye had said, that your privileges were derived from the grace and permission of our ancestors and us; (for most of them grow from precedents, which shows rather a toleration than inheritance).... So as your house shall only have need to beware to trench upon the prerogative of the crown; which would enforce us, or any just king, to retrench them of their privileges, that would pare his prerogative and flowers of the crown."

At this crisis Coke rose in Parliament and gave one of his great speeches, in which he said, "If my sovereign will not allow me my inheritance, I must fly to Magna Charta and entreat explanation of his

Majesty. Magna Charta is called *Charta libertatis quia liberos facit...* The Charter of Liberty because it maketh freemen. When the King says he cannot allow our liberties of right this strikes at the root. We serve here for thousands and ten thousands."[41]

James was furious. He told MPs "you usurp upon our prerogative royal and meddle with things far above your reach", adjourned Parliament, then told the Commons they might not discuss "matters of state at home or abroad". When they reconvened, they issued a "Remonstrance to the King" written by Coke, declaring their right to discuss anything and everything the "ancient and undoubted birthright and inheritance of the subjects of England". When James flung it back at them, they defiantly entered it into the *Journal of the Commons*.

At this point James not only dissolved Parliament, he came down and personally ripped that page from the *Journal* and threw Coke in the Tower of London. But he didn't kill him or destroy his papers. He was too shrewd to risk the uproar that would have resulted. Instead, he released Coke nine months later, and summoned one final Parliament, in 1623, that accomplished nothing with considerably less acrimony.

When James died in March 1625 the situation deteriorated rapidly. His son Charles I made Coke High Sheriff of Buckinghamshire, a post that kept him out of Parliament temporarily, and began raising money aggressively without parliamentary sanction, imprisoning without trial those who would not pay. The top courts first balked and then buckled, ruling scandalously in *Darnell's Case* in 1627 that "if no cause was given for the detention ... the prisoner could not be freed as the offence was probably too dangerous for public discussion". At this point we see again the importance of political culture, because the result was that wealthy landowners refused en masse to "lend" the king money, defying him to jail everyone indefinitely or push them to open revolt.

Charles I being insulted by Oliver Cromwell's soldiers

Instead, Charles summoned a Parliament, which predictably included many opponents including John Pym, a young Oliver Cromwell and the by now venerable Edward Coke. When Charles declared martial law and began quartering soldiers in private homes, Coke famously declared that "the house of an Englishman is to him as his castle".[42] The Commons declared that Magna Carta was still valid including its ban on imprisonment without due process. And when the House of Lords proved less resolute, the Commons led by Coke produced the 1628 Petition of Right, again making Magna Carta the cornerstone.

At a critical point in debate, with the House of Lords wavering, thinking maybe they should concede that there was a certain royal prerogative in matters of government, some leeway to govern by proclamation, Coke insisted it must all be done by rule of law in accordance with the rights of Englishmen. "Magna Carta," he reminded his fellow parliamentarians and warned the king, "is such a fellow as he will have no sovereign." The Commons passed the Petition, the Lords endorsed it, and its publication occasioned public celebrations throughout England. And we see here a clear statement of precisely the theory about popular sovereignty and the status above ordinary law of the fundamental guarantee of the people's rights that we will encounter again in the United States in 1789.

That is not to say that Charles accepted the Petition of Right. On the contrary, he determined to dispose of Parliament altogether and govern and tax without it. Coke himself had at that point retired to his estate at Stoke Poges, where he died in 1634, aged 83 and full of honours, and was buried in the family section at Tittleshall, where the inscription declares him "A Famous Pleader, A Sounde Counsellor." And indeed he was, and retired having laid the foundations not just for resistance to Stuart claims, but to resistance based on fundamental principles that would withstand not just the Civil War but the extremism of Charles I's opponents. Through a long and distinguished life, he stood on principle even when it took enormous courage and that is why there ought to be a statue of him outside every parliamentary building anywhere in the free world.

Myth vs reality

Instead he is largely forgotten. Most legislators do not know his name, and the last major biography of him was written more than 50 years ago.[43] And curiously, even most of those who value Coke's contribution to the defense of liberty in England suggest that there was more of the famous pleader than the sound counsellor in his invocation of Magna Carta as a defense of the rights of the common man. There is a broad consensus that Coke took what was essentially a forgotten medieval elite deal and reinvented it as a charter of liberties for all citizens.

Jacques Barzun, for instance, declares that "in one of the early parliamentary scuffles before the Civil War he [Sir Edward Coke] seized on Magna Carta, which was then unremembered, and smuggled into the lore about the document rights that the 13C barons had not dreamed of. (*Magna*, by the way, meant that the charter was long, not necessarily great.)"[44] How, then, was even such a famous pleader as Edward Coke able to rally the nation and the political class around it so rapidly and decisively?

As Daniel Hannan notes, many historians still "claim that Magna Carta was 'revived' in the seventeenth century, that it was conscripted to serve in a wholly unrelated constitutional dispute of that era, and that we shouldn't see it as anything more than a deal between a cornered king and his mutinous nobles – a deal that was promptly broken the moment the King could get away with it.... Yet the stubborn fact remains that Magna Carta was quoted throughout the Middle Ages in precisely the way that Whig historians were later to claim: as a defense against arbitrary government. It was seized on by the tax-weary subjects of Edward I, who forced that martial monarch to reissue it in 1297. It was cited repeatedly during the fourteenth century in the cause of baronial or parliamentary supervision of the government. A statute of 1369, during the reign of the equally martial Edward III, declared Magna Carta to have constitutional force, overriding lesser laws: 'If any Statute be made to the contrary, that shall be holden for none.' By the fifteenth century, Magna Carta had been reconfirmed by various monarchs more than forty times. The idea that Sir Edward Coke found a copy in some old collection, and gave contemporary relevance to a text that had until then been of antiquarian interest, depends upon disregarding a great deal of what was said during the intervening four centuries. It depends, too, on disregarding the most immediate practical consequence of Magna Carta, namely the establishment of an elected assembly whose duty was to hold the monarchy to its side of the bargain."[45]

It also requires disregarding the plain evidence that Magna Carta and the principles it contains were woven into the fabric of English government and constitutional law, from 1215 down to this confrontation with the Stuarts in the very early 17th century. For instance, Bracton's famous late 13th-century commentary on the laws and customs of the English[46] make very clear that the king is under the law. Magna Carta is not merely cited in the deposition of Richard II in 1399; we find numerous copies being made by monks during Richard's reign to remind people of its contents, the medieval equivalent of liking it on Facebook or retweeting it. In the mid-15th century, Sir John Fortescue, chief justice of England, went with his master Henry VI into exile and wrote his slim but influential *Praises of the Laws of England* often cited by both Coke and, later, William Blackstone, in which he again emphasizes that common law trumps statute law.

It was taken for granted in theory throughout the centuries between Magna Carta and Charles I that Parliament and the king together could not pass laws that infringed the rights of Englishmen. And the same is true in practice.

We do not only see the enactment under both John's grandson Edward I, a very formidable monarch, and Edward I's grandson Edward III, in his own right also a very formidable man, that any law contrary to Magna Carta is null and void. The institutional development of Parliament, particularly the rising influence, authority and institutional independence of the House of Commons, clearly reflects a consensus that the common people of England have a right to not just to a say in how they're governed, but fundamentally to control, to set the terms and conditions under which governments operate in England.

We see it in the deposition of Richard II, and the requirement that the new monarch Henry IV secure the approval of Parliament by agreeing to their control of the power of the purse, further refined in both 1407 and 1414. Henry VII at one point declared himself so fed up with Parliament that he would never summon another one, and would instead rule "after the French fashion".[47] But he was just venting; he reigned for 24 years and summoned seven parliaments. Not even Henry VIII was serious about ignoring it.

If people didn't mention Magna Carta every time they turned around, it's because they didn't have to. It was incorporated into the fabric both of the commentary on the law and the practice and the constitutional order. In 1559 John Aylmer, later Bishop of London but then in European exile, wrote a pamphlet urging loyalty on the English, contrasting their situation with overtaxed Europeans who "pay till their bones rattle in their skin: and thou layest up for thy son and heir."[48]

The English knew they were free, that they controlled their governments not the other way around, and they were proud of it. It's only when the Tudors and the Stuarts started challenging Magna Carta that people explicitly brought it up to block these harmful innovations and preserve their ancient rights. And in the course of doing so they were obliged to refine and formalize the procedures of Parliament that were often shockingly informal by our standards even in Coke's day. But every time fundamental rights were challenged, instead of being crushed they were forced into clearer, harder form. Including in Coke's day.

Coke didn't reinvent Magna Carta or even blow a thick layer of dust off it. If he had, it is not plausible that the nation would have rallied to him as it did, both the great and the small. It's simply that the rights in it hadn't been challenged in this way very often and when they were Magna Carta was certainly looked at, appealed to, circulated and discussed. Under the Stuarts when once again the rights of Englishmen are under siege, in a singularly determined way, it was again on Magna Carta that defenders of freedom stood.

A King Beheaded

Inigo Jones Banqueting Hall, currently undergoing much-needed renovations on Whitehall, makes it into all the architecture books, and all the history books, because it was from one of its second-story windows that Charles I stepped on the scaffold to be beheaded in 1649.

In some sense, nothing in his life became him like the leaving of it. As he was getting dressed that morning he asked for a second shirt saying it was a cold morning and he didn't want anyone to see him shiver and think he might be frightened. On the other hand, on the scaffold, he also declared: "For the people... I must tell you that their liberty and freedom consists in having of government those laws by which their life and their goods may be most of their own. It is not having share in government, sirs. That is nothing pertaining to them."[49] He defied Parliament and for that he lost his throne and his life.

In Josephine Tey's wonderful "cold case" mystery *The Daughter of Time*, investigating whether Richard III was really a monster who murdered his nephews, the hero is reflecting on iconic scenes from English history that stay in adults' memory "when tonnage and poundage, and ship money, and Laud's Liturgy, and the Rye House Plot, and the Triennial Acts, and all the long muddle of schism and shindy, treaty and treason, had faded from their consciousness." Including of course Richard III murdering the princes in the tower, with an illustration of the two lads playing, the sunlight coming through a barred window.[50]

It is not to our purpose to revive all those forgotten details today. But both ship money and Laud's Liturgy deserve brief mention because the former was one way Charles I tried to finance a then-modern government without parliamentary grants and Laud's Liturgy was his foolish attempt to remake the Church of England and impose his changes on Scotland that got him into a ruinously expensive war. The upshot was that he was forced to summon a parliament in 1640, after 11 years without one, and his confrontation with it erupted into a brutal civil war that he lost.

One critical episode in the slide into war came when Charles ordered Parliament to surrender five MPs and one Lord who he thought were colluding with his Scottish enemies, on charges of high treason. When Parliament refused, Charles personally invaded the

Commons chamber on January 4, 1642 at the head of an armed band only to find that his adversaries had been tipped off and, as the humiliated king put it, "all my birds have flown".

Charles's henchmen then forced Speaker William Lenthall from his chair and the king asked where they were. The speaker, on his knees and in imminent peril of his life, defiantly replied "May it please your Majesty, I have neither eyes to see nor tongue to speak in this place but as the House is pleased to direct me, whose servant I am here".[51] This episode explains why to this day agents of the Crown may not enter the Commons chamber, but have the door ritually slammed in their faces before the Throne Speech, a habit now approaching 400 years old, standing at as great a distance from us as that between Magna Carta and Lenthall's bravery. As Coke himself observed on more than one occasion, "out of the old fields must come the new corn."[52]

Charles did lose the Civil War and ultimately his head, ironically refusing to acknowledge the legitimacy of the court that tried him because under Magna Carta he was entitled to trial by his peers. Unfortunately, the man who replaced King Charles, Oliver Cromwell, was no friend of limited government either. He dismissed Magna Carta as "Magna Farta" and the "Petition of Right" as the "Petition of Shite," in language as vulgar as the thought behind it. And despite the elaborate institutional façade of his regime he was a tyrant whose paper constitutions, one wit aptly said, amounted only to putting a wig on the point of a sword. Indeed, he only managed to get the king executed in the first place by using his army, in "Pride's Purge," to exclude from

Parliament any moderates who would have deposed but not beheaded Charles.

Without meaning to, Cromwell did give the English an object lesson that would be repeated across the Atlantic at the state level in the period immediately after the American Revolution. By converting the legislature from a check on executive power into the sole power in the state, he made the master of the legislature unchallenged master of the state. That master was of course himself, Oliver Cromwell, a dictator whose rule was as oppressive as that of any king but less stable.

The execution of Oliver Cromwell

Cromwell went on to invade and brutalize Ireland and achieved the rare feat of uniting all the nations of Britain in hating him before dying in 1658 of malaria contracted with poetic justice in Ireland. His "Lord Protectorship" passed to his son Richard, a theoretically inexplicable reappearance of hereditary rule that, here as always, gave a revealing indication of the utter lack of legitimacy in a supposedly more democratic regime.

His son's nickname "Tumbledown Dick" gave a revealing indication of exactly how fit for high office he was considered. But Richard Cromwell showed an unexpected gift for statesmanship, recognizing his own unfitness to rule and the unsoundness of the Commonwealth and calling the so-called "Long Parliament" of the early 1640s back into session to restore the Stuart monarchy. He abandoned all pretension to rule and faded into obscurity while living until 1712, the utterly unremembered longest-lived ex-head of state in British history.

The Stuarts were duly restored in the person of Charles I's son Charles II, who promised to respect his subjects' liberties. At which point people were so bitter at Cromwell Sr. they dug up his corpse, had it hung up in chains, then beheaded. Eventually cooler heads prevailed, and it was generally agreed that Charles I, being a tyrant, had to be removed, but it should have been done in order to restore the ancient constitution, not to flee to a new form of tyranny. So in the end, Cromwell got his statue in front of Parliament, and the British got their ancient constitution and their ancient liberties back.

****

Charles II was not entirely sincere in his promises to respect liberty and govern via Parliament. Like all the Stuarts he was devious and self-centered. Indeed, he took subsidies secretly from the French king Louis XIV on the promise one day to restore England to the Roman Catholic faith. But when you shake hands with a Stuart you should count your fingers even if you too are a king, because it turned out the time was never right. Charles II took far more after his grandfather James I than his father Charles I, and carefully avoided major confrontations with Parliament and the political community because, as he characteristically put it about his years in exile between 1646 and 1660 "I am not eager to resume my travels."

When Charles II died in 1685 his brother James II took the throne and proved far more like his father than his grandfather.[53] He defied Parliament, sought to restore Catholicism, acted rashly and weakly and within four years was deposed and forced into exile in the largely bloodless "Glorious Revolution" that brought James' safely Protestant and sensible daughter Mary and her Dutch husband William of Orange to the throne as the inseparable William-and-Mary. But they were brought to the throne under another, stronger and clearer statement of the rights of Englishmen, the "Bill of Rights" of 1689. First as a declaration then as a statute, this Bill of Rights insisted on due process, forbade taxation without representation, banned standing armies within England in peacetime without parliamentary consent, protected parliamentary privilege and assured the right of Protestant citizens to bear arms.

Somehow the deposed Stuarts retained a thoroughly unmerited air of romanticism and support in Scotland that led to the Jacobite[54] risings of 1715 and 1745 about which it can only be said that these brave and loyal rebels deserved a far better cause than these wretched Stuart pretenders. But there was no serious thought of allowing anyone, even the "Young Pretender" Bonnie Prince Charlie, to rule without tight constitutional restrictions that protected citizens' liberties.

The ultimate settlement of the English Civil War was a decision that both sides had been wrong. Both Royalists and radical Parliamentarians had been far too disdainful of the ancient constitution and its institutional guarantees of orderly government and liberty, the former on behalf of the executive and the latter on behalf of the legislative branch. This recognition that there had been elements of right and wrong on both sides, and the wise "constitution of silence" that prevailed instead of energetic efforts to blame and punish all those who had been partly wrong, was based on a deep wisdom about the strength of English political culture.

The Civil War had not been a contest between the toffs on one side and the ordinary people on the other, or of pure good against pure evil. It was a war of competing ideas about the ancient constitution and to some extent of regions where different ideas tended to be stronger.

It's striking that both the first important Royalist victory and their final defeat would both have happened at Powick Bridge, in western England, the heart of Alfred's Wessex, a part of the country that was as strong for Charles I and Charles II in the English Civil War as it had been for King John in the battle over Magna Carta. It's a region that is more inclined to think of the importance of hierarchy and established rules and less attentive to abuses of power than eastern and south-eastern England where when there's an imbalance it's the other way. And curiously, as David Hackett Fischer argues in *Albion's Seed*, these two regions provided the bulk of settlers to America's old South and New England respectively and passed on their political cultures surprisingly intact.

The Founding of America

In some ways this might all seem like a lot of fuss over the history of a damp foggy island off the coast of Europe. Quaint, in some ways inspiring, giving rise to a vast tourist industry, but hardly relevant to the rest of the world.

Not so fast.

Within a few centuries of Magna Carta, the whole world would have to take note of England, as it rose to be a world power with an empire that spanned continents. And it is precisely because England's castles, cathedrals and historic sites mark the triumph of liberty against all challengers for more than a thousand years that they are worth visiting today.

The same is true of America's great historic sites, starting with the carefully reconstructed 1607 settlement in Jamestown, Virginia. The ships at Jamestown Settlement, part of the Living History Museum in Williamsburg, Virginia, give a disquieting idea of the fragility of the original three-ship expedition. The *Godspeed*, euphemistically described as the second largest ship in the fleet (it is better called the second smallest), is almost comically small, a mere 88 feet including bowsprit. But it is not the smallest; that dubious honour goes to the *Discovery*, just 66 feet long. If you take off the bowsprit it's smaller, at 38 feet, than a *Titanic* lifeboat… and a lot less sea-worthy. Crew and passengers slept in the cargo hold, with only rope netting to get up and down from the deck, no stairs. And up on the deck, the only furniture was the tiller and the pump. So if the ship was in danger of sinking, someone had to scramble up the rope netting, tie themselves to the mast to avoid being swept overboard, and pump for dear life. Yet 21 passengers and crew spent 144 days on this cockleshell of a ship.[55]

The original expedition to settle at Jamestown was horrendously ill-planned from virtually every point of view from which it was planned at all. The original colonists seemed to have had no idea what they were doing. They didn't bring proper tools, they didn't bring farmers, they knew nothing about the geography of the place they were going, they suffered from the Starving Time, terrible diseases because Jamestown was built in a swamp, another example of really, really bad planning, and they had trouble with the local inhabitants. And yet, for all the fragility of the expedition, it was solidly based at least when it comes to the principles of liberty.

The original Charter, written under the supervision of none other than Edward Coke, guaranteed to the settlers and their posterity all the "liberties, franchises, and immunities" of the English. And the settlers took for granted, without asking anyone, that those liberties included representative self-government.

Within 12 years of the ludicrous establishment of Jamestown they had set up the first representative assembly in the new world, the House of Burgesses. And while Virginia was Royalist in the English Civil War, staunchly declaring their adherence to the cause of King Charles II, in what can only be called a characteristically British piece of practical, courteous chutzpah they sent the King a pointed reminder that as Englishmen they governed themselves including on the critical point of no taxation without representation.

Unfortunately, and there's no glossing over this part of the story, the same year that the House of Burgesses was created, in 1619, in the same place, Jamestown, the first black slaves were sold in British North America. This horrendous institution, based on absolute denial of individual liberty, divided the colonies and then the United States, triggered the bloody  Civil War, and scarred and stained America to this day. Liberty is the foundation of a decent society and when you fail to respect liberty you pay a heavy price.

****

The association of Magna Carta with Virginia was not accidental or isolated. As Daniel Hannan explains, "The first Americans left these shores when the mania for Magna Carta was at its height. Magna Carta had been pressed into the contemporary quarrel between supporters of parliamentary pre-eminence and supporters of the Stuart monarchy. And the people who set up New England tended to be drawn from the parts of the country and the communities that was strongest in their belief in parliamentary supremacy. And they carried that bias, that disposition, to their new homes." Thus the attachment to Magna Carta was even stronger in Massachusetts and other northern colonies than in the South.

"It's terribly important to understand," Hannan continues "that Magna Carta to them was not an antiquarian document that they had revived and found to be relevant. It was something they carried with them, it was as much a part of their inheritance as the houses or the horses that they'd inherited directly from their parents. And so when they saw, later, as it seemed, another British monarch violating the terms, raising taxation without consent, trying people without the jury system, they regarded that as an expropriation, as a violation of the freedoms that they'd assumed they had been born with, as Englishmen."[56]

Magna Carta in the Colonies

Like Virginia, Massachusetts was devoted to liberty from the very beginning. In some ways their idea of liberty seems a bit odd even to modern New Englanders. It involved heavy community control of its members, including officials called tithingmen who spent their time meddling in how families raised their children to general approval. Such institutions did not exist in Virginia, let alone the backcountry settled closer to the revolution by rowdies from the Anglo-Scots border region including the "Scotch-Irish" who came by way of Ulster. But the heavy-handed social regulation that occurred in Massachusetts was done in the name of the freedom of Englishmen to organize their own affairs their own way. And that commitment was shared by all the colonies.

The first major settlement of Puritans took place in 1630. By 1641 there was a body of liberties, a compilation of Massachusetts laws that began by paraphrasing Magna Carta's guarantees of due process and also securing property and forbidding taxation without representation. And by 1644 there was a legislative assembly in place. To be sure, the franchise was somewhat restricted in New England in those days, but then, it was in old England too. The point is that just as in Virginia, when Englishmen reached Massachusetts they created parliaments without waiting for anybody's permission.

The Liberty Bell

The various American colonies, and regions, differed sharply from the very beginning on matters from child-rearing to criminal justice to cuisine. As Fischer's *Albion's Seed* convincingly demonstrates, these differences did not spring up in the New World but reflect habits and folkways in the different regions of Britain from which the various colonies were primarily settled. But like their various forebears, these various English people transplanted to North America were united by a love of liberty, not just in the abstract but specifically as incarnated in Magna Carta and the parliamentary institutions that grew up to protect it.

For instance the Liberty Bell, which originally hung in the steeple of the Pennsylvania State House (later renamed Independence Hall), is intimately associated in people's minds with the American Revolution.

And rightly so. But in a profound way, because the bell was originally forged to celebrate the liberties of colonial Pennsylvania, in 1751.

Pennsylvania is "the Quaker state," and the Quakers, drawn from socially excluded poor farmers from the middle hill country of the British Isles, were often at odds with the Puritans from the South-East and the Anglicans from the West, just as they had been in England. But William Penn, founder of Pennsylvania, had Magna Carta reprinted in Pennsylvania as early as 1687 specifically so that as settlers arrived from places other than Britain "the new colonists 'that are strangers, in a great measure' reached 'the true understanding of that inestimable inheritance that every Free-born Subject of England is Heir unto by birth-right, I mean that unparallel'd Priviledge of Liberty and Property.'"[57] And he warned Pennsylvania freeholders, in language that would resonate from Georgia to Maine, "not to give anything of liberty that at present they do enjoy, but take up the good example of our ancestors, and understand that it is easy to part with or give away great privileges, but hard to be gained if lost."[58]

These words could as easily have been spoken anywhere in the 13 colonies. That is why the Liberty Bell became and long remained a symbol of the aspiration for freedom. After the American Revolution, it was adopted by people pushing for the emancipation of slaves, and for the rights of women. And the original inscription from Leviticus: "Proclaim LIBERTY throughout all the land unto all the inhabitants thereof," is exactly what Magna Carta continues to do. The bell itself has not been rung since the 1840s, because it cracked. But the message has never cracked, and it still rings forth.

It certainly did in the 1760s and 1770s. It's not surprising that New England and Massachusetts in particular would be a hotbed of resistance to gathering British tyranny in the New World given Hannan's point about this region being settled by Parliamentary opponents of Charles I starting in 1630. Just how closely the settlers identified as Englishmen and with events there is underlined by the fact that over half of Harvard graduates from the 1640s saw action in the English Civil War. They came back across the Atlantic to fight, in the Parliamentary army, as stout upholders of parliamentary rights. And when, over a century later, the Puritans' descendants saw the same pattern of high-handed executive tyranny taking shape in North America, including the quartering of troops to intimidate the civilian populace, they reacted as their Roundhead ancestors had.

Thus the Boston massacre and Boston Tea Party were, obviously, in

Boston. The skirmishes at Lexington and Concord that led to full-scale warfare, Emerson's "shot heard round the world," were connected with British efforts to secure Boston by seizing colonial weapons and supplies. But while Emerson may have exaggerated

slightly, that shot was heard throughout much of the world and it was certainly heard throughout the colonies.

The result was not a replay of the English Civil War, with Roundhead Massachusetts taking on Cavalier Virginia, as the British had hoped and imagined would occur. Instead, in all the colonies the majority of politically active citizens saw it as their fight. If liberty in Massachusetts had a particular Puritan tinge, it was because Englishmen had the right to manage their own affairs in their own way. Puritans were no more inclined to ask permission to set up colleges than Virginians, or to be taxed without representation, or tried without due process. And it was to this shared spirit of liberty that all the colonies rallied when the British tried to wipe it out in Massachusetts.

****

Colonists fought proudly in the ancient tradition of British liberty. Thomas Paine's fulminations about the British constitution in *Common Sense* notwithstanding, they did not see themselves as standing aside from the sordid political history of their ancestral homeland. They were fighting for the freedom of Englishmen everywhere. And they were right. The result of their struggle wasn't just liberty in America. It helped establish liberty under law in Canada, by restoring constitutional balance and good sense where it was threatened in Great Britain.

The connection, not just to the long fight for liberty in general, but to Magna Carta in particular, was absolutely clear to the American revolutionaries. In 1765 "[t]he Massachusetts Assembly declared the Stamp Act 'against the Magna Carta and the natural rights of Englishmen, and therefore, according to Lord Coke, null and void.'"[59]

A decade later, the 1775 seal of Massachusetts, proudly displayed at the monument to the battle of Bunker Hill among many other places, shows a man with a sword in one hand and a parchment in the other. Clearly he's fighting for liberty under law. Countless statues around the world show generic books or scrolls to make a connection with law generally. But if you look closely at that particular piece of parchment, it says "Magna Charta". In their own minds, the American revolutionaries were fighting for the rights contained in Magna Carta. It was a fight for fundamental principles.

****

The Boston Tea Party Ships & Museum are a vivid recreation of that critical 1773 protest, with replica 18th-century ships from which people can throw replica 18th-century bales of tea into the harbour. It's a wonderful recreation of a wonderful event because the amazing thing about the Boston Tea Party is that it was a protest against a tax cut.

The British authorities never saw it coming because they thought people would be happy to have more money in their pockets. But the colonists' reasoning, impeccably, was this: If they can cut our taxes without our consent, it means they can change our taxes without our consent, which means they can raise our taxes without our consent, which violates the principle of no taxation without representation for which we have been fighting for more than five hundred years.

So the tea went into the harbour, the Redcoats went into Boston and the colonies rose up in a long, complicated war, albeit small-scale by modern standards, that ended with a decisive British defeat. Or perhaps not. Despite the king's dominant influence in matters of war and foreign policy into the late 18th century, there was substantial intellectual and political opposition to George III's American policy in Britain itself, and the King's defeat in America was a victory for these 'Whigs' and for freedom in Britain itself.".

The British, we tend to forget today, still defined themselves at that time primarily by the liberty at the foundation of their institutions. The proud statement that the author lived in "[a] land, perhaps the only one in the universe, in which political or civil liberty is the very end and scope of the constitution" comes not from an American rebel but from the great British legal commentator William Blackstone in 1765.[60] And he was echoing John Milton, who in 1649 had called London "the mansion-house of liberty".[61] These sentiments were still strong at the time of the American Revolution and a great many Britons saw and deplored the contrast between this tradition and the actions of their government overseas.[62]

The statesman and philosopher Edmund Burke, among others, openly opposed the effort to crush the rebellion. And in 1780, while the fighting raged and the outcome hung in the balance, a motion actually passed the British House of Commons, then heavily skewed toward the landed Tory interest by uneven representation, stating bluntly that "the influence of the Crown has increased, is increasing, and ought to be diminished."[63] In short, the executive was once again getting out of control, which was precisely what the American rebels were saying. It takes an extraordinary devotion to liberty, not just by individuals but by a political culture and system, that a resolution endorsing the adversary's superior understanding of one's own political system could pass during what was, in many respects, an Anglosphere Civil War. And indeed following the settlement of the war in 1783, the influence of the Crown was diminished in Britain, leading to the high noon of parliamentary self-government in the Victorian period before cunning politicians and party machines found a novel way to make the executive strong, which is the primary problem there, and in Canada, today.

The influence of the executive was sharply diminished in post-revolutionary America as well. The mechanisms were different but the fundamental concerns were the same. As are the troubling patterns visible in the 21st century.

The Ancient American Constitution

Independence Hall, in Philadelphia, is a monument to the genius of the American Founding Fathers in taking the essence of the British constitution and giving it a new institutional form so it would withstand the stresses that threatened to overwhelm it in the latter part of the 18th century. Once again the squeezing of liberty, instead of crushing it, forced it into a harder and sharper form. It happened again and again in the centuries following 1215. But never with more sudden and dramatic brilliance than in Philadelphia in 1787. For in that year, in that place, during a sweltering summer with the windows shut and the curtains drawn, 55 delegates gathered to write what would become the United States Constitution.

It would be understandable if the American political class had been exhausted after decades of political upheaval, military conflict, and domestic turmoil including the troubled period of unchecked legislative rule in various colonies between the Revolution and 1787. But somehow, men like Franklin, and Washington, and Madison, managed to perform an extremely creative piece of statesmanship that was a profound act of restoration not a radical act of innovation. They managed to pour the very old wine of British liberty into a striking new bottle.

They knew something had gone wrong with the traditional

George III

constitution that they had inherited. The Hanover kings, George II and George III, didn't try to crush Parliament or bypass it like the Stuarts, or govern openly as tyrants like Bad King John. Instead, they tried to seduce the legislature with perks, attractive jobs, flattery, outright bribery if it came to that, leaving the structure of Parliament intact but hollowing it out, making it a mere decorative appendage to unchecked executive rule.

So the American Founding Fathers knew they had to do something new to keep what was valuable and old alive and vital. Their solution was to produce a Constitution with a rigorous separation of powers, a Bill of Rights modeled on the 1688 British Bill of Rights but even more explicit about what government can't do, from infringing freedom of speech and freedom of religion to taking property without due process and just compensation to disarming the people, quartering troops, unreasonable search and seizure, or usurping powers not expressly granted to it. Shall not, shall not, shall not, again and again.[64]

The structure of the American Constitution also looks backward in order to look forward in a more fundamental way. Just as Magna Carta was declared to be above statute law from the time of Edward I and Edward III down to that of Charles I, so the Americans put these limits on the power of government beyond the reach of legislation so that even an executive that corrupted, seduced or deceived legislators could not override liberty even by following due process. But where the exact mechanism that put Magna Carta out of the reach of Parliament was ad hoc and obscure, relying ultimately on the very statutes that Parliament could override, the American Founding Fathers sent their Constitution to special conventions in the various states meeting for the sole purpose of voting yea or nay to a document under which, if it were adopted, the convention delegates would live as citizens rather than securing political power for themselves.

That Constitution cannot be amended by the Congress that legislates under it. Instead amendments may be recommended by Congress, but they must be ratified by state legislatures (or a specially summoned convention may recommend amendments to the state legislatures, a procedure never yet employed). It is, by design, a slow and cumbersome process that cannot be snuck past citizens or adopted in haste.

The even deeper foundation of the U.S. Constitution is the notion that rights are not something handed down from on high by a benevolent government. They are the birthright of free people, derived from natural law not man-made law.[65] It is a profoundly, deeply historically English idea. And under it governments don't need to be ordered to do something for citizens, they need to be forbidden from doing things to them. And the people must be institutionally empowered to make sure governments do not violate such prohibitions.

That is the deepest meaning of Magna Carta. And it is the deepest meaning of the United States Constitution. And it wasn't just significant for the United States. This is part of a debate and a struggle throughout the Anglosphere over the meaning of political liberty.

The American Revolution was a salutary shock in Britain, leading to a drastic curtailment of executive power that was cultural as much as institutional. And when, in Canada, there was a comic-opera revolt demanding self-government half a century later, the British gave in because they understood, again, that free men will have their rights even if they must fight for them and moreover that they should. Thus the miracle, and it is not too strong a word, that happened in the summer of 1787 in Philadelphia led to the further entrenchment of liberty throughout the English-speaking world.

Canada's Ancient Constitution

On December 7, 1837, on Yonge Street in Toronto, where Montgomery's Tavern then stood, a key confrontation occurred in the fight for self-government in Canada. The site isn't exactly the Gettysburg battlefield. Sometimes the Canadian habit of understatement can turn into a failure to commemorate historical events with appropriate dignity and it certainly has there. But the battle of Montgomery's Tavern was no Gettysburg in two other respects as well.

It was a much smaller affair, about 400 rebels facing about 1,000 on the other side, a total of four deaths, and 10 wounded.[66] But it was also unlike Gettysburg in that the losers quickly fled in disarray and the victors promptly surrendered.

William Lyon MacKenzie and his rebels retreated to Navy Island in the Niagara River where they issued a fatuously grandiose proclamation of the Republic of Canada and American sympathizers began sending supplies, money and weapons on the steamer *Caroline*. Canadian militia forces responded by seizing the Caroline, setting it on fire and sending it over Niagara Falls. Two weeks later Mackenzie took refuge in the United States where he was imprisoned for violating neutrality laws and, despite further skirmishes, the whole affair petered out.

The death of one American, misreported as the burning alive of dozens, produced a brief outcry and a protest to London from President Van Buren that was ignored. But cooler heads prevailed. In the aftermath of this minor fray, and the slightly more serious and protracted revolt in Lower Canada that saw skirmishing through 1838, over 100 dead, 29 executions and 58 deportations to Australia, the British government's response was to send Lord Durham, a.k.a. "Radical Jack," knowing perfectly well he would recommend self-government, and they would turn around and grant it, as they did with the Act of Union in 1840, the coming of responsible government in 1848, and then the British North America Act in 1867.

Despite the comic-opera feel, there was significant resistance to autocratic British rule in Canada. The reason it didn't lead to more significant conflict is that there was significance resistance to autocratic British rule in Britain also. Thus in 1837-38 they lived up to their own principles and you can see this again in Australia; when the various colonies started asking for self-government the British gave it to them, as they also did in Atlantic Canada. Australia got its independence on January 1, 1901. But there aren't any independence battle monuments Down Under because there weren't any battles.

Things are to some extent different elsewhere in the British empire, when far deeper cultural differences and a significant element of bigotry delayed the granting of self-government until the British empire was essentially too exhausted to resist after World War II. But the depth of the British commitment to due process and representative institutions is clear in the success with which so many former British colonies have sustained democracy, including in India, and the dismal failure of efforts at liberty under law elsewhere.

Fundamentally the realization that the principles of Magna Carta should apply everywhere had been recaptured after 1776, and that's why there's not much in Toronto or elsewhere to mark dramatic battles. It would still be appropriate to mark the site of Montgomery's now-vanished tavern with be a historical museum, a recreated tavern or at least a plaque, which in 2015 was absent, to remember how well things went in 1837 in this victory for liberty and common sense throughout the Anglosphere.

Part III: Challenges to Liberty

One of the most extraordinary objects in the United States Capitol, which contains its share of odd curios, is a gold replica of the original Magna Carta displayed underneath the Capitol rotunda. It was a gift from the Parliament of Great Britain to the Congress of the United States celebrating the 200th anniversary of the Declaration of Independence. And it clearly emphasizes their shared roots of liberty in Magna Carta and the rights it guarantees, and the continued relevance of that document eight centuries later. There's a gold copy of the original Magna Carta, King John's seal, an English translation of it and various emblems from British history.

This metallic document and display is that much more extraordinary when you reflect that the Declaration of Independence was against Britain. The gift was a clear acknowledgment by the British that the Americans had got it right in the 1760s, 1770s, and 1780s and they had not. The British government had strayed from its roots in liberty, and the Americans had recalled them to their good senses. The entire Anglosphere is now agreed on that.

There are subtle differences of emphasis. As Daniel Hannan explains, "Magna Carta was seen in slightly different ways from the 18th century on the two sides of the Atlantic. The way constitutional theory developed in Great Britain, Magna Carta was seen chiefly as a guarantor of parliamentary supremacy, especially after the Glorious Revolution. But in the New World, it retained the older idea of being something that stood equally above Crown and Parliament, of being, if you like, the supreme constitutional authority and that is what found its way into the debates that gave us the Declaration of Independence and then, the Constitution of the United States. It's no surprise that the three documents hang next to each other in the National Archives in Washington DC."[67]

These differences turned out to be minor indeed both in the 19th and 20th centuries. In the former, following the tumultuous upheavals of the late 18th century, then the Napoleonic Wars including the idiotic Anglosphere dust-up we call the War of 1812, you get a real golden age of liberty under law in the English-speaking world. Governments are small, due process is respected, property is protected, ownership of firearms is uncontroversial.

The result was spectacular. In this period you don't just get the

Pax Britannica, this long period of global stability during which the British navy helps stamp out the slave trade. You also get the industrial revolution in both Britain and the United States, and unparalleled prosperity for ordinary people, and remarkable cultural vitality. It is one of the most magnificent periods in the history of the English-speaking peoples.

Of course there are dark clouds. The circle of liberty was still drawn too narrowly. To some extent it excluded women. It tragically excluded Aboriginals. And of course, most ominously, in the United States it excluded black Americans. But it nevertheless showed the cultural, economic, and even military dynamism that is unleashed when people are free in orderly societies.

Gettysburg

Any sort of detailed history of the United States between 1789 and 1865 lies beyond the scope of this volume. But it was a story, as indeed the period from 1607 to 1789 was, of the flourishing of liberty under law, of the growth of representative institutions, and the extraordinary prosperity, cultural dynamism and rising geopolitical importance of this free people. Americans were quicker to grant corporations solid legal existence, more willing to listen to or at least tolerate protest movements, more ready to experiment, than almost anyone.[68] But of course they did all this while denying black Americans their most basic rights, even in the so-called "free states," and while taking land from the aboriginal inhabitants who were also coldly and deliberately excluded from the circle of protection Magna Carta drew."

As Lincoln famously observed in his second Inaugural Address, the nation paid a horrendous price for slavery. But it was not arbitrary or unjust. In immortal words carved on the wall of his memorial on the Washington Mall, he declared that "One-eighth of the whole population were colored slaves, not distributed generally over the Union, but localized in the southern part of it. These slaves constituted a peculiar and powerful interest. All knew that this interest was somehow the cause of the war.... Neither party expected for the war the magnitude or the duration which it has already attained.... Both read the same Bible and pray to the same God, and each invokes His aid against the other. It may seem strange that any men should dare to ask a just God's assistance in wringing their bread from the sweat of other men's faces, but let us judge not, that we be not judged. The prayers of both could not be answered. That of neither has been answered fully.... Fondly do we hope, fervently do we pray, that this mighty scourge of war may speedily pass away. Yet, if God wills that it continue until all the wealth piled by the bondsman's two hundred and fifty years of unrequited toil shall be sunk, and until every drop of blood drawn with the lash shall be paid by another drawn with the sword, as was said three thousand years ago, so still it must be said 'the judgments of the Lord are true and righteous altogether.'"

Gettysburg is the decisive battle in the American Civil War. And the decisive spot on the Gettysburg battlefield is the "copse of trees" still preserved today and the nearby "angle" in a low stone wall. On

July 3, 1863, Pickett's Charge reached those two positions before being driven back in desperate hand-to-hand fighting. Obviously therefore, it is sacred ground to Americans.

The Civil War caused more battle deaths than all America's other wars combined, determined whether the nation would survive or not, and whether the horrifying institution of Negro slavery would continue. But Gettysburg is not a spot of significance only to Americans.

Foreign observers from Karl Marx to John Stuart Mill understood the importance of the American Civil War to all mankind, because it was a struggle over liberty, and the meaning of liberty. Lincoln himself in the Gettysburg Address, says so: "Four score and seven years ago our fathers brought forth on this continent a new nation, conceived in liberty, and dedicated to the proposition that all men are created equal. Now we are engaged in a great civil war to determine whether this nation or any nation so conceived and so dedicated, can long endure."

Lincoln framed the war in universal terms. And both sides, in the American Civil War, were very clear that they were fighting for liberty. And except when it came to Negro slavery, the South had a very strong point about local self-government and the dangers of an excessively strong national state. The problem is, they tied all of that to an institution that was an abomination, a fundamental breach of liberty. And instead of saving slavery by tying it to local self-government, they put local self-government in jeopardy from which it has yet to recover. Because liberty underlies the American enterprise as it did Britain, and neither can flourish without it.

The Union positions at the height of the battle of Gettysburg are marked by monument after monument to the regiments who fought and whose men suffered and died there. And it's a remarkable fact about the American Civil War that it was fought, not just over liberty, but over the liberty of the most despised segment of American society. There's no getting around the fact that even in the North, there was very little sympathy for black Americans in the mid-19th century and virtually no support for social equality. And yet Americans understood in their hearts that liberty was indivisible and that it was necessary to pour out blood and treasure, to risk the destruction of the nation in order to secure the liberty under law even of people they despised.

Lincoln hoped that when the war did end, Americans would heal their nation and forget their quarrel "With malice toward none, with charity for all". But it did not happen. Vindictive northern policy and southern bitterness at the north taken out on the freed slaves ensured that this denial of liberty and its painful consequences would last another 150 years. And yet, for all that, the Civil War and its outcome is a vindication of the fundamental American devotion to freedom and the ultimate promise that, as Martin Luther King Jr. believed, it would finally be extended to all people and that "the sons of former slaves and the sons of former slave-owners will be able to sit down together at a table of brotherhood."

The institution of slavery was abolished in 1865. Tragically, the denial of legal rights to black Americans went on into the 1960s, and it was not until 400 years after the founding of Jamestown that the United States would elect a black president. But always, liberty was at the heart of the enterprise and the question of whether it is possible to build a lasting government on that basis. And that is why the Union victory at Gettysburg was a victory for the freedom of people everywhere.

More liberty

It is an astonishing fact that the Civil War could have been so devastating, to have cost perhaps 800,000 lives[69] including one-fifth of adult white males in the South, to have emptied the treasury and wasted so much production, and yet represented an almost imperceptible blip on the United States' rise to the leading industrial nation in the world by the 1890s and the leading military power as soon as it cared to be in the early 20th.

It welcomed millions of immigrants between the Civil War and World War I, and gave them unparalleled opportunities. And then came mass production and the automobile and urbanization and the jazz age and yet more disquieting, bewildering changes driven by the unleashing of enterprise and imagination that results from securing liberty under law, despite the ongoing vicious denial of rights to the non-white $1/10^{th}$ or so of its population.

The troubled history of the 20th century again lies mostly beyond the scope of this book. But it is worth noting that in three titanic struggles, the two World Wars and the Cold War, the Anglosphere came together in defense of liberty and without slighting the contributions and losses of their allies, notably the Soviets in World War II, it was these free nations who furnished the key military, economic and moral strength to defeat those threats. And they did so consciously as free people fighting for liberty.

No other banner could rally them then. And no other banner can rally them today. We may debate the meaning of rights, we may confuse genuine rights with seductive false substitutes, asserting a claim to what someone else has earned or demanding their respect regardless of our conduct. But we are free or we are nothing.

Even Franklin Delano Roosevelt's famous "Four Freedoms" during World War II contain two classic Magna Carta freedoms (speech and worship), and two modern collective ones impossible to reconcile with the older kind or, in the case of freedom from fear, to understand at all, let alone devise a sensible program for achieving via government.[70] But these deformations of our genuine tradition only underline that it is our tradition.

A Duty to Remember

A distinguished jurist, with the improbable name of Learned Hand, once said that "Liberty lies in the hearts of men and women; when it dies there, no constitution, no law, no court can save it; no constitution, no law, no court can even do much to help it."

If we do not remember it and celebrate it today it will not matter to us what happened in the past, and that's why it is so important to see that people do continue to celebrate their legacy of liberty, in Britain dedicating memorials at Runnymede (and brewing commemorative beers), in Canada where the memory of Magna Carta is preserved, and in the United States where there is an active, ongoing remembrance of liberty and of those who fought for it. The monument to the battle of Bunker Hill in Boston, for instance, is not just an impressive piece of rock. It is a place where people gather to remind themselves what their ancestors stood for, and stood shoulder to shoulder with muskets in hand for. As long as we continue to cherish the fight for liberty in the past, we will continue to wage it in the present. It's if we forget what these things mean that the monuments and the institutions will crumble around us and be forgotten.

Likewise it is no accident that people continue to flock to Independence Hall in Philadelphia, from around the United States and indeed from around the world. Or that the National Constitutional Center should successfully invite Americans and others to "see the original Bill of Rights". Because people understand that this story, the triumph of liberty, following on from Magna Carta, isn't just one way of granting rights to ordinary people. It's the only way that's ever been found. And as long as that idea is kept alive, as long as people come from Asia, from Africa, from throughout the Americas, from Europe, from Australia, to see the places where this miracle happened, then the ideas are kept alive not just in official pronouncements and chunks of granite and in trinkets, in bookmarks, in mugs to celebrate Runnymede or Bunker Hill. They stay alive in the minds of ordinary people that they ought to have rights. And as long as those ideas live, we can continue to protect our liberty from the arrogance and presumption of governments when their conceit or their carelessness would trample them.

To say so is not by any means to say that we can afford to be complacent, especially today. Millions of people each year also visit the

British Houses of Parliament which, when seen from the Albert Embankment on the opposite side of the Thames, are so pretty they should be a postcard. Indeed they very often are. But they must not be merely a postcard. And the very iconic, picturesque nature of Westminster Palace can lead us sometimes to lose sight of the fact that it's a living institution, and living institutions can sicken and die.

Even the Gothic architecture dates from the mid-19th century, in deliberate tribute to its medieval origins. Most of the original Westminster Palace, including the "Painted Chamber" dating to Saxon times, burned to the ground in the Great Fire of 1834. But it was rebuilt in this memorable style to emphasize its deep historical roots of British liberty in Magna Carta and the development of Parliament based upon the inherent rights of Englishmen contained in Magna Carta. Yet today it would be a brave, and probably unpopular, politician who would employ "medieval" as a term of praise rather than contempt. And to call Britain a land where liberty was the very end and scope of the constitution would provoke bafflement. Yet the farther Great Britain has drifted from those roots, the less great it has become.

By the same token, when Canada's Constitution explicitly declared it to be "similar in principle to that of the United Kingdom," our founders didn't just mean, "We too get cool Gothic buildings". They meant that our rights also derive from Magna Carta and from the growth of Parliament based on Magna Carta. If you actually read Canada's founding debates, you encounter repeated praise of British liberty. "I am a free man. I claim the rights and attributes of a free man, speaking in the presence of a British free assembly." "We are a free people, prosperous beyond doubt, advancing cautiously in wealth... under the British Constitution we have far more freedom than any other people on the face of the earth." "We have here a constitution for which the people nobly fought, and which was reluctantly wrung from the British government. We had the right of taxing ourselves, or legislating for ourselves."[71] Indeed, while proponents urged Confederation to preserve British liberty, opponents urged rejection of it to preserve British liberty. Nobody dismissed liberty, or disputed its British roots. That we were and must remain free, in this very specific historical sense, was not debated. It was repeatedly, even floridly, affirmed.

In 1835 Joseph Howe, the father of representative government in the colony of Nova Scotia, was tried for libeling the colonial authorities. The judge instructed the jury, correctly, that truth was not a defense under current law. But Howe appealed to them to annul the law, asking "Will you permit the sacred fire of liberty, brought by your fathers from the venerable temples of Britain, to be quenched and trodden out on the simple altars they have raised?"[72] The jury acquitted him, striking down the statute as obnoxious to liberty and hence null and void. In those days our rights were beyond the reach even of legislatures tamed by the executive.

We have to bear that in mind. We have to understand that Parliament as an effective protector of our freedom is not a picture frozen in time, it is a living institution that was under pressure in the past and only survived because of the courage of men and women of principle. And when it's under pressure today, it requires the same kind of support to remain a living institution.

Parliament is under severe pressure today. In Britain, citizens are no longer free in the way that they once were. They are over-taxed and over-regulated by parliaments too much under the thumb of the executive branch, headed in practice by prime ministers not monarchs but no less unrestrained because of it, perhaps more so because of the veneer of "democracy" that attaches to their election as Members of Parliament and head of the largest caucus in Parliament. Moreover, much law-making authority has been ceded to the undemocratic European Union.

Here in Canada the problems are at least as bad. We have not ceded sovereignty to Brussels, of course. But our parliamentarians are increasingly irrelevant in the face of an overgrown executive branch[73] and a judiciary swollen with pride and presumption. If we want our Parliament to be something more than a pretty picture out of a history book, of no relevance to the present day, we need to make sure that we too rise to the challenge of preserving those liberties that date back to Magna Carta.

Today's challenge

Despite the glittering replica Magna Carta in the U.S. Capitol, neither the British nor the American government in 1976 was true to its roots in liberty and limited government. The British at that time had punitive levels of taxation, coercive unionization, a stagnant economy and an oppressive weight of regulations and the American government too had been swollen by crises from the New Deal, prompting Franklin Roosevelt's contemptuous dismissal of a "horse-and-buggy" Constitution for the automobile era, to WWII and the Cold War and the coming of the welfare state.

It has become far worse since. The British government now regulates citizens' lives in minute detail, watches them constantly and has surrendered much of its law-making authority to the EU. In the United States, government is so big and so meddlesome the United States Department of Agriculture actively promotes the sale of fresh Christmas trees. The federal register listing new regulations, changed regulations, proposed regulations and so on, exceeds 78,000 pages a year. And recently the American Supreme Court wrote that under Obamacare the government can actually penalize citizens for not buying something the government ordered them to. All of this would outrage George Washington or William Pitt. And rightly so.

The Canadian government is no better. Extraordinarily meddlesome, extraordinarily petty, extraordinarily arbitrary. To catalogue all the ways in which our governments take property without proper compensation, limit free speech, raise revenue without recourse to Parliament, disregard due process and otherwise trample the liberties protected by Magna Carta underfoot would require a substantial separate volume. It does not matter the partisan stripe of a regime, it embraces hate speech laws, human rights tribunals, property taxes imposed by one level of government based on assessments by another, warrantless searches by executive agencies, and on and on.

It's not enough to have a gold replica of Magna Carta in your parliament. It is necessary to have it in your heart and in your institutions if you are to be true to those ideals of liberty handed down over so many centuries, which the Americans got right in 1776 and the British did not. Neither government is getting it right today, nor is ours.

We do not live under tyranny, of course. Canadians are not tortured by the state and do not vanish mysteriously in the wee hours. Rather, as Tocqueville feared, the state "does not tyrannize, but it compresses, enervates, extinguishes, and stupefies a people, till each nation is reduced to nothing better than a flock of timid and industrious animals, of which the government is the shepherd."[74]

Canadians today are overtaxed, underrepresented, and enervated by a host of petty restrictions and indignities that dictate to us that we must carry a buoyant heaving line and flashlight even when alone in a canoe at high noon. And the more we accept these things, the more the vitality inherent in a free society of responsible individuals seeps away, and the more ready we are to heed the siren song of government that if we just cede a bit more of our pesky, outdated, selfish individualism, including its constitutional protection, the better able they will be to make us healthy, wealthy and wise. But it is not so.

There is no reason to believe in principle that this tradeoff will work at all, let alone that it is worth making. There is no evidence from the history of nations where individual rights were not protected that they experienced greater dynamism, prosperity or respect for human dignity. To drift into timid servility is demonstrably unwise. And it is also profoundly unCanadian.

We are told our new collective rights, our governments unrestrained by traditional mechanisms, our vastly larger and more ambitious state are simply the final perfection of our traditional system. But the reverse is true. To quote C.S. Lewis, "It is the difference between a man who says to us: 'You like your vegetables moderately fresh; why not grow your own, and have them perfectly fresh?' and a man who says, 'Throw away that loaf and try eating bricks and centipedes instead.'"[75]

Listen to Daniel Hannan's reminder: "Unusually in the Anglopshere tradition, Parliament was seen not just as an expression of majority will, potentially even as an expression of mob rule, of tyranny of the majority, rather it was seen as an ally of the individual, and as a guarantor and defender of freedom and property. I suspect that if the authors of Magna Carta or the Civil War Parliamentarians or indeed the founders of the United States, were able to look forward at our present day, the thing that would shock them is the growth of executive power, the way in which taxes are raised, and decisions made without the consent of elected representatives, where budgets are set with only the merest parliamentary oversight and where people feel that voting doesn't matter anymore because the machinery of the central state is invulnerable to the ballot box.

"Magna Carta is a useful reminder of what freedom traditionally means. It defines our rights in essentially negative terms. If I have freedom of speech, you can't shut me up. If I have freedom of assembly, people aren't allowed to tell me who I'm allowed to congregate with or in what numbers. And it's worth reminding ourselves that that's the essential message of freedom, in an age where freedom is used to mean pretty much the opposite. It's used to mean an entitlement, a claim – the freedom to work, the freedom to have affordable health care, the freedom from discrimination and so on. Freedom, if it means anything, means a guarantee against state coercion. That's the tradition that has set the Anglosphere apart from the radical tradition of Continental Europe."[76]

****

We are part of that Anglosphere. Like our British and American cousins, we were born in liberty. We flourished under freedom. And we will cease to be true to ourselves if we cease to be free.

Such talk might seem odd in a Canadian context, when we are repeatedly told we have been devoted to big government since whenever our history began in some unspecified way that was definitely NOT AMERICAN. But this ersatz history is deeply unsatisfying, dull and uninspiring. It reminds me of a passage from *Prince Caspian*, the second book in C.S. Lewis's *Narnia Chronicles*, that "The sort of 'History' that was taught in Narnia under Miraz's rule was duller than the truest history you ever read and less true than the most exciting adventure story."[77]

Our true history is the reverse, and very much suited to inspire citizens young and old to the adventure of recapturing it.

Part of the Magna Carta exhibit

It's entirely fitting that Magna Carta toured Canada on the 800th anniversary of its original sealing. It was actually a 1300 Magna Carta and its companion Charter of the Forest, from Durham Cathedral (Durham also has a 1216 exemplar but it is too fragile to travel; even the 1300 one was so delicate it took a week just to unfold it to prepare it for travelling). But it's important to remember it's not just the velum that's fragile. It's the rights contained in Magna Carta.

As Winston Churchill wrote in his *A History of the English Speaking People* in 1956: "The underlying idea of the sovereignty of the law, long existent in feudal custom, was raised by [Magna Carta] into a doctrine for the national State. And when in subsequent ages the State, swollen with its own authority, has attempted to ride roughshod over the rights or liberties of the subject it is to this doctrine that appeal has again and again been made, and never as yet, without success."

His words offer a caution as well as an inspiration. Throughout the Anglosphere, if you take a hard look at how institutions are functioning, it's not an encouraging picture. The justice system increasingly is not accessible to everyone. It delays justice; cases take years. It sells justice; not in the sense of being corrupt but in the sense that lawyers are prohibitively expensive and proceedings go on endlessly.

A classic recent Canadian case: a bunch of plaintiffs sued the University of British Columbia because their frozen sperm was destroyed when the equipment malfunctioned. Now, what's amazing is they won the case even though they'd signed a waiver saying if the equipment malfunctioned they wouldn't have a cause for action.[78] That's not justice for UBC. But the case took over a decade and that's not justice for the plaintiffs either. And you can find stories like this throughout the English-speaking world.

Also in Canada our Supreme Court increasingly makes up law, depending on how it feels. In fact the Chief Justice explicitly said that when she hears a case, "My job is simply to listen to what the parties have to say, and to do my best to understand the position, the ramifications of deciding one way or the other, to think about what's best for Canadian society on this particular problem that's before us, and give it my best judgment."[79]

It's a vision of the judicial branch that shows remarkably little concern for what's actually in the statute books, approved by legislators elected by the people, or indeed what's in the Constitution. And so the Court takes over policy-making in areas from euthanasia to medical marijuana. Meanwhile, the executive branch – the prime minister, the cabinet, the bureaucracy – ram omnibus bills down the throats of legislators; five, six, seven hundred pages of text largely unrelated to the ostensible title of the bill. All kinds of things get crammed in and nobody knows what they say, if it even matters.

In the United States liberty is far more often praised in political discourse. But if you look at the actual functioning of its governments a different picture appears. For instance the federal Department of Justice headquarters is a sober building that fairly breathes respectability, reasonableness and respect for the rule of law. But in fact they have a prosecutorial juggernaut that rolls over defendants even if they can afford lawyers, forces them into plea-bargains because otherwise they'll spend the rest of their lives in court if not actually in jail. They even have the RICO (Racketeer Influenced and Corrupt Organizations) statute that lets the state seize your assets before you even get to trial so you can't afford a lawyer.

The principles in Magna Carta are worthy of our attention and respect. Yes we should go and see the exhibits, but we need to do more than that. We need to make sure that what it says in Magna Carta is still what happens in our institutions today and there we have a lot of work to do.

Conclusion

It's now been 800 years since the miracle at Runnymede where King John was forced to concede that free people have inherent rights. That a government that tramples those rights is no government at all. That men and women are entitled to a fair system of rules accessible to everyone, to security of the person, to protection of their property and to a say in how they're governed. This whole idea that citizens own the government, and not the other way around.

Eight hundred years is a very long time. But that doesn't mean Magna Carta is now a dusty museum piece of interest only to pedants and antiquaries. On the contrary, it's still the essential foundation of a decent society. The rights we enjoy today, the prosperity, the political liberty, the cultural dynamism, even the national security depend upon the rights it contains and on the clarity and courage of men and women who have refined those rights, expanded them and protected them tirelessly over those 800 long years.

Looking back over those eight centuries, it's astounding that Magna Carta could ever have come into existence. That the rights it contains could have been protected against all the challenges they faced, refined and expanded when they fell tragically short. That they could have been passed on to us. The rights that make a decent society possible, the only rights that have ever been found that make a decent society possible. It's an exceptional privilege to have inherited the kind of free and decent society that Magna Carta made possible. But it's also a heavy responsibility. That's why it's essential that we remember the story, that we retell the story, and that we step up now and play our part in guaranteeing the survival of those liberties for future centuries.

Postscript: Farewell to Sir Edward Coke

It was a great privilege, while making the documentary on which this book is based, to have had a chance to visit Edward Coke's tomb in Tittleshall because the truth is, I owed him an apology. Not that he needed it from me, but all my life I have been dedicated to liberty and yet, I had never heard his name until about 12 years ago.

I'd written a column about constitutional rights and a reader sent me a note saying you must be a fan of Edward Coke. And I shamefacedly admitted that I didn't know who Edward Coke was. The reader sent me a biography, Catherine Drinker Bowen's *The Lion and the Throne*, and I was electrified.

Coke is a hero to me because of his principled and courageous defense of liberty. But I was also embarrassed, for myself and an educational system in which I spent nearly a quarter of a century, because I'd never heard of him. He seems to have disappeared from the story. And that's why I say there ought to be a statue of Edward Coke on Parliament Hill, a plaque explaining who he was, what he did, and why all those who cherish their rights should honour his memory and seek to walk in his footsteps.

It was also inspiring to look out at Trafalgar Square from the roof of Canada House and see the memorials of Britain's glorious past, most notably the statue of Horatio Nelson atop its 170-foot column. But that kind of history can be intimidating as well. It's easy to feel that we could never live up to these people. I mean, look at the man, he's 10 feet tall and made of stone. We're just flesh and blood. But so were the heroes of the past.

Nelson himself was quite a character; he lived openly with his mistress back when that was considered a bit unusual, and he didn't always follow orders. At one point, during the battle of Copenhagen, the order was given with the flags on sailing ships to break off contact. He was notified of this by a subordinate, he raised his telescope to his eye, said I don't see anything. That's probably because he put the telescope to his blind eye on purpose. He went on to destroy the enemy fleet. But he also is a genuine hero.

He really was killed in the battle of Trafalgar and as he lay dying on the deck of his flagship he said the men must not know of this, because it might get them discouraged. He wanted to make sure the victory was won. That's why he has a statue made of stone, not because he was made of stone, but because he was flesh and blood who rose to the occasion. And if we remember that, we can do it too.

The death of Nelson

As Daniel Hannan said: "Think of the principles that inspired not only the authors of Magna Carta but the people who have stood for freedom and for individual rights down the history of the English-speaking peoples. The Civil War Parliamentarians, the Whigs who made the Glorious Revolution, the Founders of the United States, think of the precepts that motivated them. The idea that the legislature should be above the executive, the idea that taxes should not be passed nor laws except with the consent of our representatives. The idea that the individual is above the collective, the idea that the law is above the state. The elevation of freedom and property over raison d'état. You put them like that and they sound almost banal, almost platitudinous. But think of how easily we have allowed the machinery of government, the unelected apparatus of the central state to override our elected representatives. It's a problem throughout the Anglosphere, it's a particular problem here in the United Kingdom where we've become subordinate to the European Union and its unelected bodies. We don't need to reinvent the wheel, here. We don't need to come up with some revolutionary, radical new solution. We just need to remember who we are. Our institutions made us the freest, most prosperous, happiest and most democratic place on earth. All we should do, is honour our fathers' legacy."[80]

It was marvelous to visit Britain, but there was also for me a sense of melancholy. I wonder what has happened to Britain. It seems to me that here is the heart of a great nation but I'm not sure where the head and the limbs have gone. Somehow the British I fear have lost their way, they think that history is nothing to do with them. And I think that's because they've forgotten that at the core of their history was a passionate belief in freedom, the freedom enshrined in Magna Carta, the freedom hailed in the land of hope and glory, the freedom that Milton referred to in 1649 and Blackstone hailed in 1765.

It is liberty that made Britain great, even militarily, for as U.S. President John Quincy Adams pointed out to the United States Congress in his first annual message in 1825, "liberty is power".

As the British have lost their sense that to be British means to be free, they have become less free, they have become less great, and they have become less British. And there's a warning there for Canada: because we are offspring of what land of hope and glory refers to as the "Mother of the free". That's what it means to be Canadian, too. And if we lose it, this entire history will cease to have any meaning for us and the society that we cherish will slip away.

We must not let it happen. The challenge that confronted lovers of liberty in 1215, and in 1689, and in 1837, and at any number of points in between, and again in the World Wars and the Cold War, now confronts us. Let us answer the call.

For more information on our project, and to watch the documentary, please visit our website:
www.magnacartadocumentary.com.

Notes

[1] Specifically, the original Magna Carta in clauses 7 and 8 protected widows against forced remarriage to supporters of King John who would then acquire their property.

[2] The witan, or witenagemot, ('assembly of the wise') was an advisory council of leading citizens. Unlike modern parliaments, it had no formal rules of procedure or membership, but it represented the community and it was a foolish king who ignored its counsel.

[3] Daniel Hannan interview with the author, April 25, 2015.

[4] Daniel Hannan, *Inventing Freedom: How the English-Speaking Peoples Made the Modern World* (HarperCollins, Kindle Edition) pp. 76-77.

[5] Daniel Hannan interview with the author, April 25, 2015.

[6] Alfred reigned from 871 to 899. Around 800 AD, Viking raiders began pouring out of Scandinavia. They attacked coastal communities and pushed up rivers from Russia to France and the British Isles. Like his brothers, Alfred spent much of his reign battling them.

[7] Some quibblers insist that Canute also carries this title. It should give pause to enthusiasts for progress that both monarchs with a solid claim to this honour should both date not even to the Middle but to the Dark Ages.

[8] For good measure, he also married Matilda of Scotland, niece of the last, uncrowned Saxon king, Edgar Atheling, who led an astonishingly hazardous life before apparently dying peacefully in bed in old age.

[9] Winston Churchill *A History of the English-Speaking Peoples* A One-Volume Abridgement by Christopher Lee (Skyhorse Publishing, 2011) p. 74.

[10] Christopher Brooke *From Alfred to Henry III*, (London: Cardinal, 1974) p. 224.

[11] Bulls are named for the bulla, or seal, affixed to them.

[12] This famous or infamous incident occurred when his soon-to-be-fatal illness forced him to return from Norfolk to Lincolnshire and he sent his baggage train by a route across the tidal estuary known as "The Wash" usable only at low tide and the wagons moved too slowly and were overwhelmed by the advancing sea.

[13] Innocent III was also dead by this point, having passed away in July 1216.

[14] The 2011 movie *Ironclad* is a gripping retelling of the battle for Rochester Castle.

[15] Harold was not merely proclaimed king by the Witenagemot, he was crowned at Westminster in January 1066, though he is not considered to have reigned because he spent his time fighting off threats heroically, including at Stamford Bridge in September 1066, but ultimately unsuccessfully at Hastings the following month.

[16] Hannan, *Inventing Freedom*, p. 121.

[17] William McElwee, *The Story of England*, Third Edition (London: Faber and Faber Limited, 1968) p. 83.

[18] They were not formally readmitted until Cromwell's time, in 1655, when in a characteristically British pragmatic settlement it was determined that Edward had simply used his royal prerogative to expel a large number of individual people without establishing any general legal prohibition on Jews residing in England.

[19] Among its less intelligent aspects is the contemporary habit of denigrating radical Islamists as "medieval" as though they were about to invent the hospital, the university and parliament instead of aspiring to blow them all up, including by Britain's Prime Minister David Cameron in debating air strikes against Syria in late 2015.

[20] Matthew Spalding, *We Still Hold These Truths* (Wilmington, Delaware: Intercollegiate Studies Institute, 2009) p. 87.

[21] www.culture24.org.uk/history-and-heritage/military-history/pre-20th-century-conflict/art 487346-kings-castles-and-magna-carta-the-castles-of-the-first-barons-war as of 10/3/15.

[22] Carolyn Harris, *Magna Carta and its Gifts to Canada,* (Toronto: Dundurn, 2015) p. 75.

[23] "Magna Carta" in *The Selected Writings of Sir Edward Coke Volume II* (Indianapolis: Liberty Fund, 2003) p. 755.

[24] *Idem*, p. 762.

[25] Geoffrey Hindley, *A Brief History of the Magna Carta: The Story of the Origins of Liberty,* (London: Constable & Robinson Ltd, 2008) p. xxxii.

[26] On at least at least two recorded occasions Edward's royal treasury contained less than £3, while at one point his grandson Edward III had to pawn his crown.

[27] Curiously, kings could sometimes determine the outcome by naked threats of mayhem against Parliamentarians. But even in those cases, MPs insisted on adhering to appropriate procedure, preserving their institutional integrity to fight another day and, it turned out, win decisively over time.

[28] Edward III had five sons who lived to adulthood, a source of parental pride no doubt but also the cause of great dynastic complications resulting eventually in the bloody and ruinous "Wars of the Roses" between the Lancasters descended from John of Gaunt, Duke of Lancaster, and the Yorks descended both from Edmund's fourth adult son Edmund of Langley, Duke of York and the only surviving child, Philippa, of his second adult son Lionel of Clarence.

[29] "Procedure Regarding Money Grants, 1407" in William L. Sachse, *English History in the Making,* (Toronto: Blaisdell Publishing Company, 1967) p. 151.

[30] The specific institutional issue was that if the only thing that elevates Magna Carta above statute law is a statute, it can be undermined in a two-step process beginning by repealing or overriding its statutory protection, as indeed did eventually happen in Britain.

[31] Norman Davies, *The Isles,* (New York City: Oxford University Press, 1999) p. 415.

[32] Douglass C. North and Robert Paul Thomas, *The Rise of the Western World,* (New York City: Cambridge University Press, 1973) p. 121.

[33] Eugene F. Rice, Jr., *The Foundations Of Early Modern Europe, 1460-1559,* (New York City: W.W. Norton & Company, Inc., 1970) p. 93.

[34] Christopher W. Brooks, "The Ancient Constitution in Sixteenth-Century Legal Thought" in Ellis Sandoz, ed., *The Roots of Liberty,* (Indianapolis: Liberty Fund, 1993) p. 94n.

[35] Moreover, as noted below, justice in Coke's day was better than ours in key respects including affordability and resolution of cases at a reasonable pace instead of dragging on for years or even decades.

[36] Charles Howard McIlwain, *Constitutionalism: Ancient and Modern,* (Indianapolis: Liberty Fund, 2007) p. 96.

[37] Harris *Magna Carta and Its Gifts to Canada,* p. 62.

[38] Specifically, according to tradition, some variant of "Who will rid me of this troublesome priest?" to which four drunken knights raised unsteady hands then hoisted sail for England; Henry was in the ancestral French lands he regarded with at least as much affection as England.

[39] This writ should be revived and used against integration into the European Union.

[40] Catherine Drinker Bowen, *The Lion and the Throne: The Life and Times of Sir Edward Coke 1552-1634* (Toronto: Little, Brown and Company, 1956), p. 251.

[41] *Idem,* p. 453.

[42] Hence Coke's influence on posterity is clearly visible in the famous 1763 declaration by William Pitt the Elder that "The poorest man may in his cottage bid defiance to all the forces of the crown. It may be frail, its roof may shake, the wind may blow through it, the storm may enter, the rain may enter – but the King of England cannot enter."

[43] It's Bowen's *The Lion and the Throne* and it remains well worth reading.

[44] Jacques Barzun, *From Dawn to Decadence: 1500 to the Present 500 Years of Cultural Life.* (NY: Perennial, 2001), p. 266.

[45] Hannan, *Inventing Freedom,* pp. 116-117.

[46] Henry de Bracton was a cleric and judge under Henry III in the late 13th century.

[47] Paul Johnson, *The Offshore Islanders: A History of the English People* (London: Phoenix, 1995) p. 111.

[48] Alan Macfarlane, *The Origins of English Individualism* (Oxford: Blackwell, 1979), pp. 178-79; Aylmer scathingly continues "They go from the market with a salad: and thou with good flesh fill thy wallet."

[49] Bowen, *The Lion and the Throne,* p. 476.

[50] Josephine Tey, *The Daughter of Time,* (Markham: Penguin Books Canada, Ltd., 1954) p. 33.

[51] Wikipedia, September 9, 2014.

[52] *The Selected Writings of Sir Edward Coke Volume I* p. 173.

[53] Indeed, Charles had long regarded his brother as a strange kind of trump card; when James warned Charles about lack of security his brother retorted "they'll not kill me to make you king".

[54] To the dismay of generations of schoolchildren, the name "Jacobite" for these reactionaries comes from the Latin form of James "the Old Pretender", son of James II (James VI to pointed Scots nationalists) is almost identical to "Jacobin," the name for the most extreme radicals in the French Revolution.

[55] Interestingly the *Discovery* was later part of the Arctic expedition in which Henry Hudson's crew mutinied and set him adrift, never to be seen again.

[56] Interview with the author, April 25 2015.

[57] Harris, *Magna Carta and its Gifts to Canada,* p. 81.

[58] David Hackett Fischer, *Albion's Seed,* (New York City: Oxford University Press, 1989) p. 597.

[59] Harris, *Magna Carta and its Gifts to Canada,* p. 82.

[60] William Blackstone, *Commentaries of the Laws of England Vol. 1* (Chicago: The University of Chicago Press, 1979) p. 6.

[61] Eric Foner, *Give Me Liberty! An American History Volume I* (2nd Seagull Edition, New York City: W.W. Norton & Co., 2009) p. 79.

[62] Indeed, British commanders in America appealed to the colonists to adhere to the crown precisely, if implausibly, to preserve their "ancient constitution" of liberty.

[63] Bruce Lenman, *Integration, Enlightenment, and Industrialization; Scotland 1746-1832* (Toronto: University of Toronto Press, 1981) p. 72.

[64] Much of the binding text is in the Bill of Rights, not part of the original Constitution but part of a deal to get it ratified by assuring the anti-Federalists that what Federalists felt was secured implicitly in the actual Constitution, by virtue of not granting these powers to the federal government, would be spelled out explicitly.

65 As Carolyn Harris notes, "when lawyer Silas Downer dedicated a 'liberty tree' in Providence, Rhode Island, in 1768, he declared, 'The great charter of liberties, commonly called Magna carta, doth not give the privileges therein mentioned, nor doth our Charters, but must be considered only declaratory of our rights, and in affirmance of them.' According to Downer, Magna Carta represented natural law and could not be superseded to justify new taxes or contrary legislation." (*Magna Carta and its Gifts to Canada* p. 81.)

66 Also, be it noted, a clash of armed citizens in both camps, at a time when people debated who was right but not whether they should be armed.

67 Interview with the author, April 25, 2015.

68 The main exception is the British, who launched the industrial revolution, imposed the *Pax Britannica* and dominated the world militarily, economically and culturally with a government that took perhaps 10 per cent of GDP, left citizens unmolested, and didn't even have compulsory schooling until 1870.

69 The standard figure of just over 600,000 military deaths is over a century old and undercounts significantly.

70 The other, freedom from want, has justified an enormous expansion of government throughout the Western world including the Anglosphere without, we are assured by activists, achieving anything resembling its lofty if nebulous goal.

71 All these quotations are from Janet Ajzenstat, *The Canadian Founding: John Locke and Parliament* (Montreal & Kingston: McGill-Queen's University Press, 2007) p. 50.

72 Dennis Gruending, ed., *Great Canadian Speeches* (Markham: Fitzhenry & Whiteside, 2004) p. 7.

73 The increasingly bloated cabinets now found at both the federal and provincial level represent an executive absorption of the legislature's more ambitious and talented members that would deeply impress George III. It is not unknown for more than half the "treasury benches" to be ministers, secretaries of state and so on today.

74 Tocqueville, *Democracy in America* Vol. II Book 4 Chapter 6.

75 Clive Staples Lewis, *The Abolition of Man* (London: HarperCollins, 1999) p. 29.

76 Daniel Hannan, interview with the author, April 25, 2015.

77 Clive Staples Lewis, *Prince Caspian* (London: Lions, 1980) p. 170.

78 *National Post* May 20 2015 p. A1.

79 Quoted by Gordon Gibson in *National Post* June 10 2015 p. A11.

80 Daniel Hannan, interview with the author, April 25, 2015.